LONDON
The Cubby
2024 Long Weekend Guide

James Cubby

NO BUSINESS HAS PAID A SINGLE PENNY OR GIVEN *ANYTHING* TO BE INCLUDED IN THIS BOOK.

Fisher Collins Press

London

The Cubby
2024 Long Weekend Guide

TABLE OF CONTENTS

Chapter 1
WHY LONDON?

London is one of my favorite cities to visit. A city thriving with history and the location of scores of films (with lots of film location tours like Harry Potter). The West End offers incredible theatre and I often spend a week in London just to see theatre. Shopping in London is topnotch with classic shops like Harrods and Selfridges. I like to hit the boutiques and the many vintage shops for designer duds at bargain prices. There's something for everyone in London. They say, "In London, everyone is different, and that means anyone can fit in."

"Why, Sir, you find no man, at all intellectual, who is willing to leave London. No, Sir, when a man is tired of London, he is tired of life; for there is in London all that life can afford."

Samuel Johnson said this to James Boswell when they were discussing whether Boswell's affection for London would wear thin should he choose to live there, as opposed to the zest he felt on his occasional visits. (Boswell lived in Scotland and visited only periodically. Some people are surprised to learn that

Boswell and Johnson were far from inseparable over the last twenty years of Johnson's life, the period Boswell knew him.)

This discussion happened on September 20, 1777, and Johnson, who had an unusual fear of being alone, was always going out and enjoying what London had to offer. I couldn't agree more wholeheartedly with Johnson, and his observation of the London of 1777 is just as apt today.

Chapter 2
GETTING ABOUT

THE UNDERGROUND

People have been using the Underground, more commonly known as the Tube, since 1863. This is a public metro system that serves a large part of Greater London as well as parts of the counties of Buckinghamshire, Hertfordshire and Essex. The Underground has 270 stations.

While it's possibly the best means of transportation when considering area covered, speed and reliability, there are a few disadvantages. In the summer it's hot and crowded and is not a place you want to be stuck on a summer's day and it's become a bit pricey for visitors to use. While I used to use the Tube quite often when I lived in London during most of the 1980s, I don't use it as much when I'm on short visits, preferring the speediness and comfort of taxis. I also prefer the bus to the Tube.

If you are planning on using the Tube, you should plan your journey and try to avoid rush hour. Check out the Journey Planner on the Transport for London website - www.tfl.gov.uk - where you will find the quickest route to your destination. Check the notice boards at each station for travel information, delays and updates. Wait until those leaving the train have exited before getting on. Always check your ticket and make sure that you have purchased the correct ticket for your destination and that it covers all zones that you will be traveling through. Make sure that you are going to the correct platform as many stations have multiple platforms. (Example: Euston station has six platforms for two underground lines.)

Greater London is served by 12 Tube lines that run between 5 a.m. and midnight, Monday to Saturday, with reduced operating hours on Sunday. Fares vary depending on times and zones so if you're traveling on the Tube you should consider purchasing an **Oyster Card** or a **Travelcard** to get the best fares and not have to stand in the lines. (Note: You don't want to be caught on the Tube without a valid ticket because you're liable for an immediate fine.) Pick up a London Underground map at any London Tube station or a London Travel Information center.

TAXIS

A visit to London is not complete without a ride in one of the city's black cabs, the official cabs of London. These iconic symbols of London, with their unusual round shape, were originally designed to comfortably transport a gentleman wearing a bowler hat. The cabs may be hailed on the street or booked in advance for door-to-door service. Cabs have yellow TAXI sign on the roof of the vehicle and when illuminated the cab is available.

Only hail a cab on the street if you are not near a "rank," the term Londoners use for their cabstands. At a rank, cabs and passengers line up allowing the first in line to be served. Black cabs can be booked in advance by phone or online at www.londonblackcabs.co.uk

Unlike many US cab drivers, London cab drivers are quite knowledgeable. In fact, I think they're the best cabbies in the whole world.

Potential cabbies must pass an exam that requires them to have extensive knowledge of London including memorizing over 25,000 streets and 320 routes so when you travel by cab, your driver is not only an excellent source of information, be assured you won't get lost and will get to your destination by the best route available. Black cabs can accommodate up to five passengers, including luggage, at no extra charge. All cabs are wheelchair accessible and guide dogs ride for free. Tipping isn't required but is expected.

MINICABS

Minicabs are not available on the street and must be booked in advance. Most hotels and hostels will have a list of reputable and licensed cab operators. Minicab drivers do not have the vast knowledge required of black cab drivers so they are not experts on streets and routes. The advantage to taking a minicab is the price. While they are cheaper than black cabs, you must negotiate the price when booking your ride. Beware: there are minicabs that will offer you rides on the street at cheaper rates but realize that these are unlicensed cabs and you do not want to get into an unlawful vehicle.

BUSES

One of the best ways to see London is on the famous red double-decker buses. The red buses offer great sightseeing opportunities while you're getting around London. London boasts one of the largest networks of buses with approximately 7,500 iconic red buses. These buses travel all over London with 19,500 bus stops and stations. There is a flat fare throughout the bus network but the fares are cheaper with a pre-paid Oyster Card. Travelcards are accepted on all buses. Most buses require you to buy tickets before you board so you must purchase tickets at the machines located next to the main bus stops. London buses run all night so bus service is available after the Tube closes. Check bus-stop information boards for route info. For more information on routes and schedules visit these sites: www.tfl.gov.uk or www.londonbusroutes.net

BY CAR

London has an excellent public transportation system which makes it the quickest way to get about. I definitely recommend you NOT drive in London for several reasons.

One, many are not used to the fact that the British drive on the "wrong side" of the road and the driver sits on the right side of the car. This takes a bit of readjustment and can be tricky particularly at peak times. Most cars are manual transmission and that's what you'll be given at any rental company unless you make a reservation for an automatic. Drivers must abide by all the rules of London and all drivers must wear seatbelts. It is also very difficult to find parking space in London and parking can be very expensive. A non-UK driving license is valid in Britain for up to 12 months from the date of your last entry. For full details of the legal requirements for drivers visit the Department for Transport website: www.tfl.gov.uk.

BY BICYCLE

Seeing London by bike is not only great exercise but also an economic way to explore the city. Visit the Transport for London website for cycle routes - www.tfl.gov.uk All bikers must wear helmets. There are several companies that rent mountain or hybrid bikes – deposits are required. **The London Bicycle Tour Company** (www.londonbicycle.com) rents bikes at reasonable rates and offers daily bike tours of London. Another way to rent bikes is through **Barclays Cycle Hire**, called Boris Bikes after Boris who was mayor of London when the project was launched, which has more than 8,000 bikes and over 550 bike docking stations around the city. The system is fairly easy, just hire a bike, ride it, then return it at any docking station. Bikers need a debit or credit card to register. Folding bikes are allowed on all Tube lines, river services, local trains, the Docklands Light Railway and London's Tramlink without restrictions.

MOTORBIKES AND SCOOTERS

If you're going to travel the streets of London by motorbike or scooter be aware of all driving rules and remember that you're driving on the other side of the street. Bikers must wear helmets. Also note that many of the roads are narrow, busy and congested even during non-peak driving times. There are benefits to riding a motorbike or scooter in London and many commuters choose bikes over cars. With a motorbike you can travel through traffic faster, avoid public transportation, and it's easier to find parking. There are several outlets offering rentals such as Motorcyle**Hire**Uk www.motorcyclehireuk.com.

GETTING TO AND FROM THE AIRPORT

HEATHROW AIRPORT
Heathrow Airport, located to the west of Central London, handles more international passengers than any other airport in the world. With 5 busy terminals filled with a variety of shops, restaurants, information counters, and exchange facilities, this airport can seem a maze with its crowds of incoming and outgoing passengers. All arrivals can be found on the ground floor of Terminals 1, 3, 4 and 5. All arrivals must go through passport control, baggage reclaim and Customs. Departures can be found on the first floor of Terminals 1 and 2, the ground floor of Terminal 3 and the top floor of Terminal 5. Remember that all passengers must first go through security control before entering the departure lounge. Always double check the Heathrow website to confirm your terminal.

Traveling by Car
Heathrow is located approximately 17 miles west of central London. If you're traveling by car, most of the trip can be made via the M4 motorway but avoid traveling during peak periods as it can get congested. The airport is also near the M40 and M3 and Terminal 5 can be reached directly from the M25. There are ample parking facilities at Heathrow; however, each car park has their own rules and rates.

Car rental centers are located along the northern edge of the airport with free shuttle buses available from all terminals. Beware of the long lines at the hire desks (satellite rental services) and if you arrive during early morning or late evening you may have to take a shuttle bus and check out your rental at the depot. If you are driving to the center of London be warned that you will be liable for the Congestion Charge (£8 per day during weekdays between 7am-6pm). Note that automatic number plate recognition cameras are actively looking for violators and your car rental company will bill you with the £30 fine if you fail to pay.

Public Transportation

London's public transportation system is very good and most of the travelers heading to Central London use public transportation. All Heathrow terminals have public transport links to and from Central London including buses, rail services and London Underground. Heathrow has five different rail stations for the five terminals so make sure that you take the right train as not all trains got to the same terminals. www.**tfl**.gov.uk

By Rail

Trains are a comfortable way to travel to and from the airport as they are quite modern with air-conditioning and Free Wi-Fi access on board. The Heathrow express is the fastest way to travel from Central London to Heathrow and back. The express departs from Terminal 5 every 15 minutes and makes stops at Terminals 1 & 3 then runs non-stop to London Paddington, Central London. The traveling time is approximately 15 minutes. Trains run from Heathrow from 5:42 a.m. until 11:42 p.m. Check the website for schedule and rates. www.heathrowexpress.com

By London Underground

The most economical way to travel to Heathrow Airport from London is London Underground's Piccadilly Line. Travel time is less than an hour and the wait time is never more than ten minutes. Heathrow has three London Underground stations: one for Terminals 1 and 3 and one each for Terminal 4 and Terminal 5. All stations are in Travelcard Zone 6. Fares vary depending on how you pay and it's recommended that travelers use Oyster and Travelcards. Remember that the Tube is a rapid transit system designed with short journeys in mind and if you're traveling with luggage this may not be the most comfortable choice. Almost all the stations involve negotiating staircases and escalators. www.tfl.gov.uk

By Bus

The N9, the night bus, runs approximately between the hours of 11:59 p.m. and 5 a.m. This bus runs every 20 minutes to Central London (Trafalgar Square). Travel time is approximately 75 minutes. Standard fares apply and the Oyster Card is accepted. www.tfl.gov.uk

By Taxi

Traveling to Heathrow from London by black cab is easy as the cabbies have extensive knowledge of the terminal. Just book a cab in London, making sure they are aware of your departure time, and your journey will be carefree. Arrivals landing in Heathrow should take note that there are plenty of taxis lined up for customers. Only use a black cab or a reputable minicab. Never use unauthorized drivers. All Heathrow Terminals have an approved taxi desk and stand where taxis can be booked.

HOTEL

Chapter 3
WHERE TO STAY

AIRBNB.COM
www.airbnb.com

Investigate the scourge of hoteliers everywhere in the world, this site that alerts frugal travelers to bargain lodgings in people's homes almost anywhere in the world. You might find a flat a block from Champs Élysées that's a third of the price of a small room at the Georges V and with a lot more charm.

Voilà!

You will need to do your research, but the good thing is that you pay Airbnb.com directly, not the person hosting you.

They get protections from you (if you're a crazy person and trash the host's apartment, you will pay dearly) and you get protection from them (in case they offer something not available in the rental).

All in all, a wonderful meeting of the minds for savvy travelers looking for bargains and people in cities where travelers want to go who want to maximize the revenue potential of that spare room.

I frequently stay in an Airbnb in SoHo near making all the theatres walkable. Choose your favorite location so you can walk.

I have several friends of mine who do this in Miami, on South Beach where I live, and they are all happy with the entire experience.

3 SOUTH PLACE

3 South Pl, London, +44 20 3503 0000
www.southplacehotel.com
NEIGHBORHOOD: Liverpool Street
This 80-room, luxury hotel features Conran-designed interiors, two restaurants, and three bars. Guests can select from five room categories This service-oriented hotel offers luxurious amenities like: 40" Bang & Olufsen TVs with over 40 channels (including Sky Sports) and free movies on demand, fully stocked mini-bar, and on-site gym. Conveniently located to Moorgate and Liverpool stations as well as incredible shopping, great restaurants and nightlife.

20 NEVERN SQUARE
20 Nevern Square, London, +44 0 20 7565 9555
www.20nevernsquare.com
NEIGHBORHOOD: Earls Court
This luxurious boutique four-star luxury hotel offers 20
beautifully designed rooms with a mix of European and Oriental
influences. Amenities include: 24-hour room service, health &
fitness club by arrangement, same day laundry & dry cleaning,
free Wi-Fi, free morning newspapers, and airport transfers. The
hotel is conveniently located near the Earls Court Exhibition
Centre and Earl's Court London Underground Station.

45 PARK LANE
45 Park Ln, London, +44 20 7493 4545
http://www.dorchestercollection.com/en/london/45-park-lane
NEIGHBORHOOD: Mayfair
Offering guests a relaxed and luxurious experience, this hotel
boasts contemporary interiors and spacious guestrooms and
suites. Guests can climb the beautiful central staircase to the first
floor for **Bar 45** or dine at **CUT at 45 Park Lane**, Wolfgang
Puck's first restaurant here. Hotel amenities include hotel fitness
studio (open 24/7), in-room beauty treatments, and access to the
facilities at the Dorchester Spa

BROWN'S

33 Albemarle St, London W1S 4BP, +44 20 7493 6020
www.roccofortehotels.com/hotels-and-resorts/brown-s-hotel/
NEIGHBORHOOD: Mayfair

I've stayed frequently here at Brown's, one of London's finest 5-star hotels that has a certain "lived in" feeling that's hard to describe. With 117 rooms and 29 suites, you can expect luxurious accommodations. Amenities include Free shuttle to and from airport, Fitness Center, cozy fireplaces, and luxurious beds with Hypnos-brand mattresses. The **Donovan Bar**, hotel's on-site bar, offers a beautiful contemporary meeting spot. Afternoon Tea is served in the award-winning English Tea Room. The hotel spa has an impressive menu of treatments. The HIX Mayfair restaurant offers sophisticated elegance and a top-notch menu.

BULGARI HOTEL & RESIDENCES, LONDON

171 Knightsbridge, London, +44 20 7151 1010
www.bulgarihotels.com/
NEIGHBORHOOD: Knightsbridge

Located on the edge of Hyde Park, this luxury hotel offers accommodations in a contemporary setting with top-notch service. The hotel offers 85 beautiful, appointed guestrooms and suites. Hotel facilities include: a full gymnasium and physical training center, 11 spa treatment rooms, a 25-meter swimming pool, a 47-seat cinema, a stunning ballroom, and a Cigar Shop and sampling lounge. Amenities include mini-bar, large bathrooms, 42" LCD TVs, free wireless access, and Nespresso coffee machine. On-site bar (Il Bar), Spa with 11 treatment rooms, and 25-meter swimming pool.

CAFÉ ROYAL
10 Air St, London, +44 20 7406 3333
www.hotelcaferoyal.com
NEIGHBORHOOD: Soho
Located in the heart of central London, this luxury 5-star 160-room hotel is a beautiful historic landmark. The hotel also boasts six historic suites. The hotel features a variety of restaurants and bars including the Tea Room that offers British informal all-day dining. The iconic **Grill Room**, with restored Louis XVI décor and detailing, is the ideal place to enjoy Champagne, cocktails or nibble on the menu of British snacks. Also onsite is the Akasha Holistic Wellbeing Center an urban retreat offering a gym, lap pool, Watsu pool, sauna and Hammam/steam room with a menu of signature treatments. Amenities include luxurious bed linen, fully stocked Butler's Pantry and Bang & Olufsen media systems, 24-hour room service, free daily newspaper and wireless high-speed Internet.

CHARLOTTE STREET HOTEL
15-17 Charlotte St, London, +44 20 7806 2000
www.firmdalehotels.com
NEIGHBORHOOD: Fitzrovia
Located just north of Soho, this 52-room hotel features a "Bloomsbury Group" theme throughout the hotel displaying original art from the period. Amenities include WiFi, flatscreen TVs, and iPod docking stations. Hotel facilities include Fully equipped gym, concierge, private dining and meeting rooms, guest drawing room and library, DVD library, state of the art screening room and on-site restaurant (OSCAR).

CLARIDGE'S

49 Brook St, Mayfair, London W1K 4HR, +44 20 7629 8860
www.claridges.co.uk
NEIGHBORHOOD: Mayfair
This iconic luxury 5-star hotel, Mayfair's Art Deco jewel,
features beautiful suites, grand event spaces and delicious
cuisine. Conveniently located near shopping districts, parks and
business center. Elegant rooms and suites available. Amenities
include gift pack on arrival, 24-hour room service, iPod docking
stations, Selection of on-site restaurants and bars, health club &
spa. Elegant afternoon tea service. Hotel gift shop.

CORINTHIA HOTEL LONDON

10 Whitehall Pl, London, +44 20 7930 8181
www.corinthia.com/en-gb/london
NEIGHBORHOOD: Westminster
This grand Victorian building offers guests luxurious
accommodations with 294 guestrooms, 40 are Suites and 7 are
Penthouses. The hotel offers two elegant restaurants, The
Northall and **Massimo Restaurant & Oyster Bar** as well as
three bars. This opulent hotel features amenities like free WiFi
access, state of the art media hubs in every room, 24-hour room

service dining, and an on-site wellness spa with an impressive menu of treatments.

COVENT GARDEN HOTEL
10 Monmouth St, London, +44 20 7806 1000
www.coventgarden.london/place/covent-garden-hotel
NEIGHBORHOOD: Covent Garden
Located in the heart of the theatre district, this hotel offers 58 guestrooms and suites. Amenities include WiFi, flat screen TVs, iPod docking stations, 24-hour room service, fully stocked minibar, and Miller Harris bath products. Hotel facilities include gym, guest drawing room and library, restaurant and bar, state of the art screening room, DVD library, and body & treatment room. Conveniently located near Soho, attractions like the Royal Opera House and some of London's top restaurants, bars, cafes, nightlife and shopping.

DORCHESTER
53 Park Lane, London W1A 2HJ, +44 20 7629 8888
www.dorchesterhotel.com
NEIGHBORHOOD: Mayfair

This five-star hotel is on the list of the world's most iconic hotels and offers a truly English experience. Located in the center of London overlooking Hyde Park, this hotel offers luxurious accommodations, a beautiful spa, and award-winning cuisine.

Alain Ducasse at The Dorchester serves the ultimate in French cuisine. I well remember my first experience in this restaurant. My landlady at the time was French. I rented a mews flat in West Kensington from her. She had done some favors for me and by way of thanks, I asked her to choose "a nice little French restaurant" and I would take her and her husband to dinner. When the cab pulled into the Dorchester, I almost fainted. When I got the bill, I think I did.

Amenities include Bang & Olufsen flat-screen TVs, a Bose radio/CD player, a Philips keyboard and a combination fax, scanner and copier, and luxurious white marble bathrooms with the deepest baths in London.

DORSET SQUARE HOTEL
39-40 Dorset Square, London, +44 20 7723 7874
www.firmdalehotels.com/london/dorset-square-hotel
NEIGHBORHOOD: Marylebone
Located in London's West End, this hotel is conveniently located near shopping, bars and restaurants. The Dorset offers 38 individually designed guestrooms, many looking out on the private garden square. The guest drawing room and The Potting Shed bar & restaurant are open all day. Amenities include WiFi, iPod docking stations, safe, minibar, and flat-screen LCD TVs. Day passes at the local Fitness First Gym are available as well as in-room spa services.

THE HARI
20 Chesham Pl, London, +44 20 7858 0100
www.thehari.com/
NEIGHBORHOOD: Belgravia
This hotel is a fine example of the Thompson Hotels luxury experience. Marked as the most luxurious boutique hotel in Belgravia section of London, this 85-room hotel offers beautiful top-notch accommodations featuring bold architecture and design. Hotel facilities include: an 80-seat restaurant, an intimate

library bar, and a fitness center. Amenities include WiFi access, outdoor terraces, 24 hour in-room dining, and State-of-the-Art Fitness Center.

HAZLITT'S

6 Frith St, London, +44 20 7434 1771
www.hazlittshotel.com
NEIGHBORHOOD: Soho
Located close to Soho Theatre, this four-story Georgian hotel was built in 1718. Furnished with antiques, this beautiful hotel offers old fashioned hospitality and efficient service. The rooms are comfortably furnished in vintage décor. Guests are served breakfast every morning in their rooms which includes a freshly baked croissant. Amenities include: 24-hour room service, same day dry cleaning and laundry service.

THE LONDON EDITION

10 Berners Street, London, W1T 3NP, +44 20 7781 0000
www.marriott.com/hotels/travel/loneb-the-london-edition
NEIGHBORHOOD: Fitzrovia
Like the rest of the EDITION Hotels, this hotel located in an iconic landmark building offers luxurious accommodations, excellent dining and entertainment with modern services. The 173 guestrooms and suites feature oak floors and wood-paneled walls. The hotel features a bar, a tavern and a cocktail bar. Berners Tavern at The London EDITION offers an impressive British menu. Amenities include: 24-hour gym, free high-speed Wi-Fi access, valet parking, and free workstation complete with Apple computers.

MAIN HOUSE

6 Colville Rd, London, +44 20 7221 9691
www.themainhouse.co.uk
NEIGHBORHOOD: Notting Hill
This luxury hotel offers beautiful suites that occupy an entire floor of a period Victorian house furnished with antiques. Amenities include Free wireless Internet connection, TVs, and free newspaper with morning coffee or tea is delivered to room. Conveniently located close to the world-famous Portobello

Road, antique markets, designer shops, galleries, restaurants, theatre, and nightlife.

MANDARIN ORIENTAL HYDE PARK
66 Knightsbridge, London, +44 20 7235 2000
www.mandarinoriental.com/london
NEIGHBORHOOD: Hyde Park
Known as one of London's most celebrated hotels, guests enjoy elegant and luxurious accommodations. The stylish hotel is home to two of the city's best restaurants and a gorgeous spa. The hotel overlooks Hyde Park and is conveniently located near Sloane Street, Harrods, Royal Albert Hall and South Kensington's museums. The hotel features 173 guestrooms and 23 individually-decorated suites. The Royal, Imperial and Presidential Suites offer butler service.

ME LONDON
336-337 The Strand, London, 1 (929) 207-1033
www.reservations.com/hotel/me-london
www.melia.com/en/hotels/united-kingdom/london
NEIGHBORHOOD: Strand
This hotel offers 157 beautifully designed rooms including 16 suites. Hotel facilities include two New York restaurants (**Cucina Asellina** and **STK London**), Roof Bar with an outdoor terrace and spectacular views of London and Marconi Lounge. Amenities include: 24-hour gym, high speed Wi-Fi, atmospheric lighting, DVD/CD, in-room spa menu, integrated digital media hub, and answering machine via the TV. Conveniently located near attractions like Covent Garden, Trafalgar Square, Houses of Parliament and St. Paul's Cathedral as well as theatres, shopping, restaurants and nightlife.

MILESTONE HOTEL

1 Kensington Ct, London, +44 20 7917 1000
www.milestonehotel.com
NEIGHBORHOOD: Kensington

You know immediately that you're in a five-star hotel when your butler takes you on a tour of the hotel's facilities, shows you your room and hands you a glass of Champagne. The lovely facilities include **Cheneston's Restaurant**, the **Stables Bar**, the Conservatory and the Lounge. Guests can select from deluxe guest rooms, luxurious suites or apartments. Amenities include heated resistance pool, gym, sauna, chauffeur-driven Bentley, spa treatment room, 24-hour butler service, fully stocked mini-bar, iPods and docking stations in every room, Free wireless Internet, and DVD/CD players. Pet friendly.

NO 5 MADDOX STREET

5 Maddox St, London. +44 20 7647 0200
www.living-rooms.co.uk
NEIGHBORHOOD: Marylebone
This stylish, boutique hotel, ideal for the modern traveler, offers
one-, two- and three-bedroom suites with 24-hour concierge.
Amenities include Shopping services, free welcome tray, in-
room spa treatments, free membership to local private gym, and
Flatscreen TV / SKY / DVD / MP3 docking station in every

suite. Guests receive free Artisan du chocolat chocolates on arrival.

NUMBER SIXTEEN
16 Sumner Pl, London, +44 20 7589 5232
www.firmdalehotels.com/london/number-sixteen
NEIGHBORHOOD: South Kensington
Located close to the Victoria & Albert and Natural History Museums, this hotel offers comfortable lodging that ideal for travelers hoping to see the sites. This 41-room luxury hotel boasts its own tree-filled private garden. Amenities include: 24-hour room service, valet, concierge, high speed wireless Internet access, fully stocked mini-bar, DVD/CD player, Flat Screen TVs, iPod Docking station, and Miller Harris bath products. Tea is served all day.

THE RITZ
150 Piccadilly, London, +44 20 7493 8181
www.theritzlondon.com
NEIGHBORHOOD: Piccadilly
Known as the hotel that sets the grade for all others, this hotel
even operates with a dress code in certain areas of the hotel.
Formal dress is required when dining in The **Palm Court** and
during lunch and dinner service in The Ritz Restaurant. The
Rivoli Bar is more relaxed. The luxury hotel offers impressive
guestrooms designed in the lavish Louis XVI "house style."
Amenities include free high-speed broadband and Wi-Fi

Internet access, 24-hour room service, free shoe-shine service,
free porter service, free daily newspapers and LCD TVs. The
Palm Court serves Afternoon Tea, the quintessential English
experience.

SHANGRI-LA HOTEL, AT THE SHARD

31 St Thomas St, London, +44 20 7234 8000
www.shangri-la.com
NEIGHBORHOOD: London Bridge
Located on the 34th to 52nd floors of Renzo Piano's iconic building, this elegant hotel is Shangri-La's first property in the UK, with 202 luxurious guestrooms and suites. On arrival, you're treated to a cup of Chinese tea at **TING** on level 35 before heading to your room. Hotel facilities include the stylish **GŎNG bar** on level 52, which offers wonderful views of the city. Amenities include infinity pool, free high-speed Internet, and Acqua Di Parma bathroom products. Conveniently located near attractions like the Tate Modern and Westminster Abbey.

THE SOHO HOTEL
4 Richmond Mews, London, +44 20 7559 3000
www.firmdalehotels.com/london/the-soho-hotel
NEIGHBORHOOD: Soho
Located on a quiet street in the heart of the entertainment
district, this hotel offers 91 individually designed guestrooms,
suites, and apartments. This red brick hotel offers a loft-like
experience, as all the guestrooms feature floor to ceiling
windows. Amenities include WiFi, flat screen TVs, iPod
docking stations, and movie-screening rooms. Hotel facilities
include hotel bar (winner of Best Hotel Bar in 2011), fully
equipped gym, and spa facilities with a menu of treatments.

Chapter 4
WHERE TO EAT

10 GREEK STREET
10 Greek St, London, +44 20 7734 4677
www.10greekstreet.com
CUISINE: Modern European
DRINKS: Full Bar
SERVING: Lunch, Dinner, closed Sundays
PRICE RANGE: $$$
NEIGHBORHOOD: Bloomsbury
This small eatery offers a small seasonal menu with dishes like
Filet of Halibut and Brecon Lamb cutlets. Menu favorite was the
Scallops and chorizo. Cocktail list includes several variations on
the negroni. Nice wine selection. Tables placed very close
together. No reservations. Closed Sundays.

AKOKO
21 Berners St, London, +44 20 7323 0593
https://akoko.co.uk
CUISINE: West African
DRINKS: Full Bar
SERVING: Lunch on Sat & Dinner Wed to Sat
PRICE RANGE: $$$

NEIGHBORHOOD: Fitzrovia
Fine dining eatery offering 5-course menus of West African cuisine. Rotating menus. Things I've enjoyed on past visits: creamy Nigerian pumpkin soup with bites of lobster, a sprinkling of nutmeg, served with puffed wild rice. Onion stew with lemon and BBQed quail. Impressive wine pairings. Reservations recommended.

ALAIN DUCASSE AT THE DORCHESTER

Park Lane, Mayfair, 020-7629-8866
www.alainducasse-dorchester.com
CUISINE: French
DRINKS: Full Bar
SERVING: Lunch, Dinner
PRICE RANGE: $$$
NEIGHBORHOOD: Mayfair

This is a lavish restaurant serving French haute cuisine in the luxurious setting of one of London's finest hotels. You feel a little like a titled aristocrat just walking through the lobby. Well, I do, anyway. More Michelin stars have been given to Ducasse than almost any other chef, and he certainly deserves every one of them. Though the hotel is ornate and elaborate, the restaurant itself is quite modern with an entirely contemporary vibe. The jewel of the restaurant is the stunning 'Table Lumière'—this is a semi-private room surrounded by 4,500 shimmering fiber optics dropping dramatically from the ceiling. This is like an expensive shower curtain, to put it bluntly, and encircles the round table where a handful of customers are then secluded from the rest of the room, except that they are right in the middle of it and you can see partially through this moving, living curtain of light. The table is set with Hermès China, gorgeous flatware and Saint-Louis crystal. I find the effect of this table to be a little tacky. The fact that it's in the middle of the room and so completely emphasized is what turns me off. It's as if you're in coach class if you're on this side of the barrier and whoever's on the other side of that glittering curtain is in first class. Not that I didn't want to join them, mind you. Favorites: Pasta cannelloni, the turbot with green almonds and Seared Foie Gras. This is very upscale dining with a dress code. Book ahead.

THE ANCHOR & HOPE
36 The Cut, London, +44 20 7928 9898
www.anchorandhopepub.co.uk
CUISINE: British cuisine
DRINKS: Full Bar
SERVING: Lunch & Dinner
PRICE RANGE: $$
NEIGHBORHOOD: Southwark, Waterloo
Gastropub with an ever-changing menu of modern British fare. The good thing is this place is always packed because the vibe is so cool and the food so good. The bad thing: this place is always packed. Favorites: Dover sole and Lamb shoulder. Try the Poppyseed cheesecake for dessert. You can eat in the dining room or in the bar.

Angler outdoor seating

ANGLER
3 South Place, Finsbury, 020-3215-1260
www.anglerrestaurant.com
CUISINE: British (Modern)
DRINKS: Full Bar
SERVING: Lunch, Dinner
PRICE RANGE: $$$$
NEIGHBORHOOD: Finsbury
Elegant eatery located seven floors up with a seafood-focused menu. This is a popular foodie place and boasts not only a Michelin star, but a killer rooftop terrace with spectacular views. Favorites: Cured sea bass and Roast Newlyn cod. Vegetarian friendly. Impressive wine list with over 250 labels. Incredible views. Reservations recommended.

Angler

AULIS
16-a St Anne's Ct, Soho, 020-3948-9665
www.aulis.london
CUISINE: European / British cuisine
DRINKS: Full Bar
SERVING: Lunch, Dinner

PRICE RANGE: $$$$
NEIGHBORHOOD: Soho
Popular among foodies, this eatery offers the ultimate,
interactive dining experience in a little hole in the wall you'll
love. It's exclusive dining with only eight seats available. All
dishes are cooked in front of you because there's no room to do
it anywhere else, the place is so small, and everything is
carefully explained, sometimes in excruciating detail. The staff
here are so serious, one wants to tell them to lighten up, but they
are committed. The menu is ever-changing, and it really matters
not what they serve. It's always beyond excellent. Be sure to opt
for the wine pairings that are offered. Reservations only (book
way ahead). This is owned by the same team behind
ROGANIC, and they do a lot of experimenting on dishes here.
It's rather difficult to get into, as you can imagine, but well
worth a try.

AVE MARIO
15 Henrietta St, London, +44 7933 624393
https://www.bigmammagroup.com/en/accueil
CUISINE: Italian
DRINKS: Full Bar
SERVING: Lunch & Dinner, Weekend Brunch
PRICE RANGE: $$$
NEIGHBORHOOD: Covent Garden
Popular Italian eatery offering a menu of meat dishes, pizza,
pastas, and desserts. Favorites: Filetto Allo Rossini (English beef
with home-made pâté de foie) and Ave Mario's Autumn
Tagliata (Chargrilled bavette steak – serves 2).

BARBARY

16 Neal's Yard, Seven Dials, London, **no phone**
www.thebarbary.co.uk
CUISINE: Middle Eastern / Mediterranean
DRINKS: Full Bar
SERVING: Lunch & Dinner
PRICE RANGE: $$$
NEIGHBORHOOD: Covent Garden

Small eatery (24 numbered seats at the horseshoe-shaped bar where all the action occurs) with a menu of small plates. Focus is cooking with fire, either grilling over coals or baked in clay ovens the way they used to do it hundreds of years ago. (OK, thousands of years ago.) Very hip little place. The music is electro-pop, but not so loud you can't talk. Good alone or for a couple. A party of 4 makes it tough. You wait at a drink rail for your number to come up, but you can order drinks and snacks while you wait. When you get to a bar stool, ask your neighbors what they ordered and try something new and different. You'll be glad you did. Favorites: Arayes (pita pouches grilled and stuffed with seasoned beef & lamb—you'll scarf these down);

Cauliflower Jaffa; Lamb Cutlets with cumin crust; Pata Negra neck (pork). Extensive wine list.

BARRAFINA
43 Drury Lane, Covent Garden, +44 20 7440 1456
10 Adelaide St, Covent Garden
26-27 Dean St, Soho
www.barrafina.co.uk
CUISINE: Spanish
DRINKS: Full Bar
SERVING: Lunch, Dinner
PRICE RANGE: $$$
NEIGHBORHOOD: Covent Garden
This popular Spanish eatery in 3 locations offers a delicious assortment of Mallorcan and Barcelona style tapas and other Spanish dishes. Menu favorites include Grilled chicken thighs with romesco sauce and Coca Mallorquina. Nice selection of wines by the glass. Reservations not accepted so expect a wait. Don't go after 2 p.m. for lunch or you won't get served.

BENARES
12a Berkeley Square House
Berkeley Square, 020-7629-8886

www.benaresrestaurant.com
CUISINE: Indian
DRINKS: Full Bar
SERVING: Lunch, Dinner
PRICE RANGE: $$$$
NEIGHBORHOOD: Mayfair
This is an upscale eatery serving Indian-British fusion cuisine.
Here you'll find Indian cuisine elevated to the Michelin star
level. Utterly exquisite food prepared and served impeccably.
You can choose from a pre-theatre prix fixe menu or large plates
suitable for sharing or opt for the a la carte menu, which is very
comprehensive. Favorites: Lamb cutlets with a lovely spiced
rub; and Chargrilled Scottish Salmon with lemongrass couscous.
There's a daily special menu that's well worth a glance, and a
Vegetarian menu is offered as well. Extensive wine list. Creative
cocktails like the zingy Passion Fruit Chutney martini. I know
how awful that sounds, but try it, you'll like it. Reservations
recommended.

BLACK AXE MANGAL
156 Canonbury St, London, **no phone**
www.blackaxemangal.com
CUISINE: Turkish
DRINKS: Full Bar
SERVING: Dinner Mon – Sat, Brunch Sat & Sun.
PRICE RANGE: $$
NEIGHBORHOOD: Islington
Small simple eatery offering a menu of Turkish-inspired dishes.
It's a tiny place that seems even smaller because of the heavy

metal music blasting away. Nothing "romantic" about this place, but it is fun. Staff is hip, youngish, tats and t-shirts, and you can tell they *like* this music. A few small tables but try to snag a seat at the bar where you watch a master at work pulling food from the "mangal grill." Favorites: Lamb offal flatbread; Rabbit in a crispy breading; and Bone marrow flatbread. Nice selection of ales. They take reservations.

BRAWN
49 Columbia Rd, London, +44 20 7729 5692
www.brawn.co
CUISINE: Modern European
DRINKS: Full Bar
SERVING: Lunch, Dinner
PRICE RANGE: $$$
NEIGHBORHOOD: Shoreditch
Lovely restaurant - ideal setting for a date night. Popular eatery on Columbia Road (widely known for its flower market on Sunday) offering Mediterranean small plates menu. They're focused on using local products whenever possible, like pork belly from Suffolk. The menu is quite impressive with choices like Mozzarella & Ratatouille, and Cheese Souffle. And of course, their famous selection of meats. Tiramisu fans will delight at the giant squares of tiramisu served for dessert. Serious wine list. Reservations recommended. Other Favorites: Squid & black pudding and Oxtail. Good house wine and wine list. (The wines are mostly all natural.) Menu changes nightly.

CAT & MUTTON
76 Broadway Market, London, +44 20 7249 6555
www.catandmutton.com
CUISINE: British cuisine
DRINKS: Full Bar
SERVING: Lunch & Dinner
PRICE RANGE: $$
NEIGHBORHOOD: Broadway Market, London Fields
Traditional gastropub with daily specials and weekend DJ sessions. Favorites: Lamb shoulder and Beer battered Haddock & chips. Nice selection of beers on tap (16) and in bottle (20).

Sunday roasts are popular serving excellent Bloody Mary's. Wednesday night is quiz night.

CEVICHE PERUVIAN KITCHEN & PISCO BAR
17 Frith St, London, +44 20 7550 9364
https://cevichelondon.com/
CUISINE: Peruvian
DRINKS: Full Bar
SERVING: Lunch, Dinner
PRICE RANGE: $$$
NEIGHBORHOOD: Soho
This tiny restaurant serves authentic Peruvian dishes and fresh ceviche. Menu favorites include Quinoa Salad and Peruvian Corn Cake. Ceviche is made right in front of you at the Ceviche Bar so you know it's fresh. Ceviche also serves delicious signature cocktails and a nice selection of creative desserts.

CHILTERN FIREHOUSE
1 Chiltern St, London, +44 20 7073 7676
www.chilternfirehouse.com
CUISINE: British; European
DRINKS: Full Bar
SERVING: Breakfast, Lunch, Dinner
PRICE RANGE: $$$

NEIGHBORHOOD: Marlybone

There's counter service, high-top tables, cozy booths if you want privacy, in this brightly decorated spot at the Chiltern with an open kitchen that lets you see the cooks at work. The Chiltern was one of the first purpose-built firehouses in London, and dates to 1889. Andre Balazs converted it into 26 exquisitely furnished rooms served by a staff trained to pamper you. You will fall in love when you first walk into the cozy lobby. Go for the Vichyssoise with razor clam, Grilled Welsh Lamb Rump with collard greens, Wild Turbot Crudo. Menu changes weekly.

CIRCOLO POPOLARE

40-41 Rathbone Place, London, no phone
https://www.bigmammagroup.com/en/trattorias/circolo-popolare
CUISINE: Italian/Mediterranean/Pizza
DRINKS: Full Bar
SERVING: Lunch & Dinner, Weekend Brunch
PRICE RANGE: $$$
NEIGHBORHOOD: Fitzrovia

Sicilian trattoria offering a varied menu of Italian favorites, Napolitano pizzas, daily-made pastas, and desserts. Favorites: Mafaldine with truffle & mascarpone cream and Gnocchi with mushrooms & cheese sauce. Great cocktails.

CLARIDGE'S RESTAURANT

Claridge's, Brook St, London, +44 20 7629 8860
www.claridges.co.uk
CUISINE: British
DRINKS: Full Bar
SERVING: Lunch, Dinner, closed Sundays
PRICE RANGE: $$$$
NEIGHBORHOOD: Mayfair

If you're looking for a 5-star experience in an Art Deco gem, this is your place. Top-notch menu of treats like truffle, lobster and citrus baked alaskas. The crowd is fancy, the food is traditional and expensive but it's an experience worth the money (if you can afford it). Reservations recommended.

THE CORAL ROOM

Bloomsbury Hotel
16-22 Great Russell St, Bloomsbury, London, +44 20 7347 1221
www.thecoralroom.co.uk
CUISINE: British cuisine
DRINKS: Full Bar
SERVING: Lunch, Dinner
PRICE RANGE: $$$
NEIGHBORHOOD: Bloomsbury
Beautiful lobby bar located in the hotel offering an elegant country house décor. Great cocktails but also an elegant setting for breakfast, coffee or light snack (like the Dorset crab on toast). Live music most evenings.

CLAUDE BOSI AT BIBENDUM
Michelin House, 81 Fulham Rd, 020-7581-5817
http://bibendum.co.uk
CUISINE: French (Modern)
DRINKS: Full Bar
SERVING: Lunch, Dinner
PRICE RANGE: $$$
NEIGHBORHOOD: Chelsea
This is yet another upscale eatery, but this one's on two levels offering two distinct dining experiences. On the ground floor is a seafood and oyster bar and on the floor above you find French Haute Cuisine. You'll be very impressed with the floor-to-ceiling-stained glass windows offering great views of the busy streets outside. Menu picks: Cornish Turbot and Line-caught Cornish Cod.

THE CLOVE CLUB
380 Old St, London, 020-7729-6496
https://thecloveclub.com
CUISINE: British
DRINKS: Full Bar
SERVING: Lunch, Dinner
PRICE RANGE: $$$
NEIGHBORHOOD: Shoreditch
Set in the glamorous former Shoreditch Town Hall, this upscale
eatery features a seafood focused menu that emphasizes seasonal
produce that comes from all parts of the country. Though the
setting is slightly informal, there's nothing informal about the
high-level quality of their Michelin-starred food. Favorites:

Scottish Spider Crab Hot Pot and Raw Orkney Scallop, which has become their signature dish. The scallops come from the Orkney Islands off the northeastern coast of Scotland. (Very nippy weather up in these parts, I can tell you from first-hand experience when I spent a bit of time up there drinking whiskey day in and day out. It's so cold up there it's no wonder the Scots drink so much. But I'm forever thankful to the Scots for drowning me in their fabulous spirits.) This dish—I'm back to the scallops—is prepared with Perigord truffles, hazelnuts and clementine or mandarin—unbelievable flavors. You'll get to choose from different prix fixe tasting menus. All are fine in what's come to be known as one of the best restaurants in the world. Impressive wine and cocktail list. Book ahead.

CORA PEARL
30 Henrietta St, Covent Garden, 020-7324-7722
www.corapearl.co.uk
CUISINE: European / British cuisine
DRINKS: Full Bar
SERVING: Lunch, Dinner
PRICE RANGE: $$$
NEIGHBORHOOD: Covent Garden
Located in a chic Convent Garden townhouse, the menu focus is comfort food elevated to a new level. Favorites: Fish Stew & Croutons and Tamworth Pork Chop, with Celeriac & Bordelaise. You must try the French fries here; unlike any you've had

before. They are cut thick and look a little stumpy, but the flavor is out of this world. Book ahead. This is a perfect choice for pre-theatre dinner. Oh, you might be interested in the name Cora Pearl. It's well worth reading the Wikipedia entry on this woman, which I did on my iPhone when I made my first visit here—she was a famed Parisian prostitute who reached the height of her fame as a courtesan in the 1860s. She wasn't French at all, but English, born Eliza Emma Crouch but had a fascinating career once she realized what she was cut out for. I meant to ask why they named this restaurant after the woman, but I was so taken by the food and wine and the fun-loving crowd that I completely forgot.

CORE BY CLAIRE SMYTH
92 Kensington Park Rd, Notting Hill, 020-3937-5086
www.corebyclaresmyth.com
CUISINE: French / European / British
DRINKS: Full Bar
SERVING: Lunch, Dinner
PRICE RANGE: $$$$
NEIGHBORHOOD: Notting Hill
Fine dining in a comfortable setting. British food served at its best, but I found quite a few European influences on this menu, most of them French. The chef here is the first and only, I might add, female chef to win 3 stars from the folks over at Michelin.

As you can see, she's quite celebrated. The décor is sleek, modern, with clean lines and flattering lighting. There's a lovely bar where you can sample some of their creative craft cocktails made to exacting standards. Favorites: Isle of Mull Scallop Tartare and Roasted Monkfish. Vegetarian, Vegan and gluten-free options. Reservations recommended.

CUT
45 Park Lane, London, +44 20 7493 4545
www.45parklane.com
CUISINE: American / Steakhouse
DRINKS: Full Bar
SERVING: Brunch, Lunch, Dinner
PRICE RANGE: $$$
NEIGHBORHOOD: Mayfair
This restaurant is the European debut of chef and restaurateur Wolfgang Puck with a menu that reflects the award-winning Beverly Hills counterpart. A simple menu features signature prime steaks and fresh seafood along with Puck's version of American classics. Classic cocktails and a well-crafted wine list. Dining room seats 70 with Bar 45 seating 30.

DARJEELING EXPRESS

2a Garrick St, London, +44 20 3375 3772
www.darjeeling-express.com
CUISINE: Indian
DRINKS: Full bar
SERVING: Lunch & Dinner, Lunch only on Sundays; closed
Mon & Tues
PRICE RANGE: $$$
NEIGHBORHOOD: Covent Garden
So popular, you need to make reservations far in advance, so
plan. The women in the kitchen are not trained chefs in this
family-owned eatery but know their stuff just as well as anybody
who went to school (better, even). No such thing as a bad dish
from the items on the single page menu offering excellent Indian
"home cooking." Favorites: Spiced mutton kabobs; Murgh ka
Saalan (boneless chicken thighs) and Goat Kosha Mangsho
(slow cooked Bengali goat curry).

DEAN STREET TOWNHOUSE

69 - 71 Dean St, London, +44 207 434 1775
www.deanstreettownhouse.com
CUISINE: British cuisine
DRINKS: Full Bar
SERVING: Breakfast, Lunch, Dinner, Afternoon Tea

PRICE RANGE: $$$
NEIGHBORHOOD: Soho
Located in Soho, this hotel features an all-day dining room with an incredibly long bar and the feel of a private-members-club dining room. The menu features typically British seasonal fare. Menu favorites include Twice Baked Smoked Haddock Soufflé and Braised Veal Cheeks. Check out the hotel's diverse art collection while you're there with over 60 works of art by artists like Paul Noble, Keith Tyson, Peter Blake, Tracey Emin and Keith Coventry.

THE DELAUNAY
55 Aldwych, London, +44 20 7499 8558
www.thedelaunay.com
CUISINE: British cuisine / Modern European
DRINKS: Full Bar
SERVING: Breakfast, Lunch, Dinner, Afternoon Tea
PRICE RANGE: $$$$
NEIGHBORHOOD: Convent Garden
Inspired by the grand old European cafes, this eatery provides a great dining experience and a décor featuring green leather banquettes, antique mirrors and a marble floor. Menu favorites include Chicken Curry (often a dish of the day) and Smoke

Salmon. You must try the house-baked Austrian cakes. Nice
wine list.

DINNER BY HESTON BLUMENTHAL
66 Knightsbridge, London, +44 20 7201 3833
www.dinnerbyheston.com
CUISINE: British cuisine
DRINKS: Full Bar
SERVING: Dinner
PRICE RANGE: $$$$
NEIGHBORHOOD: Hyde Park
Located in the **Mandarin Oriental**, this place offers a truly
unique dining experience. The menu features historical dishes
(pulled from old British cookbooks) like meat fruit (Mandarin,
chicken liver & foie gras parfait, grilled bread). Other menu
favorites include Chicken oysters and Grilled octopus. Excellent
food, creative cocktails and nice wine pairings. Interesting
desserts with choices like the Tipsy Cake - a segmented brioche
soaked with icing glaze and served with spit roasted pineapple.
Reservations recommended.

THE DRAPERS ARMS

44 Barnsbury St, London, +44 20 7619 0348
www.thedrapersarms.com
CUISINE: British cuisine
DRINKS: Full Bar
SERVING: Lunch & Dinner
PRICE RANGE: $$
NEIGHBORHOOD: Islington
Popular gastropub with a pub feel featuring high ceilings, chandeliers and checkerboard floor. Check out their special events like the American Style BBQ held on July 4th (they even added a few American beers for the day). Favorites: Leg of Lamb. Menu has something for everyone including vegetarian selections. There's a nice garden during good weather.

THE DUKE

7 Roger St, London, 020 7242 7230
No Website
CUISINE: Pub Fare
DRINKS: Full Bar
SERVING: Lunch & Dinner; closed Sundays
PRICE RANGE: $$
NEIGHBORHOOD: Bloomsbury
Quiet pub with Art Deco décor featuring a nice menu of authentic British fare. Charles Dickens lived just a few feet away around the corner. Favorites: Cod Filet and Duke's Homemade Burger. Menu changes weekly except for a few favorites like fish and chips.

E. PELLICI

332 Bethnal Green Rd, London, +44 20 7739 4873
www.epellicci.co.uk
CUISINE: Italian
DRINKS: No Booze
SERVING: Breakfast, Lunch
PRICE RANGE: $
NEIGHBORHOOD: Bethnal Green
Popular with locals, this place is a great stop for breakfast. The Full English breakfast includes grilled stem mushrooms, grilled

tomato halves, sausage, bacon, and a thick slice of toast with an egg over easy.

EVELYN'S TABLE
The Blue Posts, Cellar, 28 Rupert St, London, +44 7921 336010
https://www.theblueposts.co.uk/
CUISINE: Contemporary
DRINKS: Full Bar
SERVING: Dinner: Closed Sun & Mon
PRICE RANGE: $$$
NEIGHBORHOOD: Piccadilly Circus

A reservations only 10-seat counter dining experience in the basement. Book well in advance because there are only these few seats. It's quite well worth the trouble. Nightly offering includes 5 courses and wine pairing. Favorites: Cornish Mackerel with gooseberry & elderflower and Dried-aged Duck. Menu is kept secret until arrival.

St. James's Market

FALLOW
52 Haymarket, London, +44 20 8017 1788
https://www.fallowrestaurant.com
CUISINE: British
DRINKS: Full Bar
SERVING: Lunch & Dinner: Closed Mon
PRICE RANGE: $$$
NEIGHBORHOOD: Mayfair
Contemporary eatery offering a creative menu of locally sourced ingredients. Favorites: Lamb tongue grilled; Pork neck with sage; Cull Ewe mutton chop; Fresh Brill with mussels. Lots of interesting Vegetarian options. Reservations required.

FORZA WINE AT THE NATIONAL THEATRE

National Theatre, Upper Level, 133 Rye Ln, London, +020 7732 7500
https://forzawine.com/
CUISINE: Small Plates
DRINKS: Full Bar
SERVING: Open everyday noon – 10:30 p.m. National Theatre closed on Sundays
PRICE RANGE: $$
NEIGHBORHOOD: South Bank

Here's a pre-theatre (and after) dining choice. Located on the top floor of the National Theatre, this popular eatery (you'll be lucky to get a seat on the patio during warm weather) offers a small plate menu. Three plates for two people should do it but this is a place where you can actually order everything on the menu (£140 including 4 desserts). Popular dishes include Cauliflower fritti and aioli, Potato, pancetta and pickled cabbage, and Onglet, braised shallots and horseradish. They have creative cocktails like a Watermelon Martini.

FRYER'S DELIGHT

19 Theobalds Rd, London, +44 20 7405 4114
No Website
CUISINE: Fish & Chips
DRINKS: No Booze

SERVING: Lunch, Dinner
PRICE RANGE: $
NEIGHBORHOOD: Bloomsbury
This cozy little locals' favorite serves up a no-frills menu. Menu favorites include Cod flakes and Rockfish. Great bread slathered in butter.

GAME BIRD
The Stafford
16-18 St James's Place, London, +44 20 7493 0111
www.thestaffordlondon.com
CUISINE: British
DRINKS: Full Bar
SERVING: Lunch & Dinner
PRICE RANGE: $$$$
NEIGHBORHOOD: St James's, Green Park
Located in the elegant Stafford Hotel, this upscale eatery offers a thoroughgoing tour of solid British fare. I used to nip in here when I visited my shirtmaker whose store was just around the corner. (In fact, it still is.) Never disappointed. It's a bit on the

posh side, traditional, old-school, but thoroughly charming and soothing. If you've ever wondered what one of those "gentlemen's clubs" is like, come into the American Bar (with its tons of memorabilia hanging from the ceiling) and peek into the Game Bird to find out. That's what this place feels like. Favorites: Venison Wellington and Chicken & Duck liver parfait. Vegetarian friendly. Impressive wine list.

GLORIA

54-56 Great Eastern St, London, +44 7903 540051
www.bigmammagroup.com
CUISINE: Italian
DRINKS: Full Bar
SERVING: Breakfast, Lunch, & Dinner 7 days
PRICE RANGE: $$$
NEIGHBORHOOD: Liverpool Street / Broadgate
Upscale and yet extremely comfortable eatery offering Italian classics. The interior is over-decorated on purpose, filled to the point of bursting with knick-knacks, kitschy stuff, decorative plates lining the walls, plants hanging from the walls, peach-colored upholstery, comfy-loungy seating that feels more like sofas than banquettes. All designed to make you feel at home. Favorites: Carbonara (with the pasta tossed in a hollowed-out

wheel of Pecorino); and Truffle pasta. Nice tiramisu. Note that it's open for breakfast, so brunch here on weekends is a sure bet.

THE GREENHOUSE
27-A Hay's Mews, 020-7499-3331
https://www.greenhouserestaurant.co.uk
CUISINE: French - Haute
DRINKS: Full Bar
SERVING: Lunch, Dinner
PRICE RANGE: $$$$
NEIGHBORHOOD: Mayfair
This luxurious eatery serves traditional French cuisine. The place is exceptional in every way, and fully justifies its 2 Michelin stars, which puts it on a par with the very best spots in London. When the weather is nice, there's nothing finer than to make your way down the garden path that leads to the dining room. The stone artwork you see in the garden is by British sculptor Emily Young. Each dish—and I mean each and every one—is so artfully and meticulously prepared that you'll wonder if you should destroy the masterpiece by eating the damn thing. Trust me, you'll eat it. My Menu picks: Caviar with Cornish Crab and succulent Veal Sweetbreads (from Limousin) served

with tasty, puffed buckwheat. Exceptional wine list with over
3,400 labels. Reservations recommended.

GYMKHANA
42 Albemarle St, London, +44 20 3011 5900
www.gymkhanalondon.com
CUISINE: Indian
DRINKS: Full Bar
SERVING: Lunch & Dinner; closed Sundays
PRICE RANGE: $$$
NEIGHBORHOOD: Mayfair
The look here is reminiscent of an Englishmen's sporting club
set in the British Raj. Popular eatery with tasting menu. Lots of
Indian favorites like Chicken Butter Masala or suckling pig
vindaloo. If you're not familiar with Indian cuisine you may
have to ask for explanations but the staff is friendly and the food
is good.

HAKKASAN
8 Hanway Place, London, +44 20 7927 7000
www.hakkasan.com
CUISINE: Chinese
DRINKS: Full Bar

SERVING: Lunch, Dinner
PRICE RANGE: $$
NEIGHBORHOOD: Fitzrovia
Founded in London in 2001, this is the original restaurant of the Hakkasan brand that has now spread all over the world. Here you'll find a new twist on the Chinese fine-dining experience. The dark English oak decorated restaurant features an open kitchen. Menu favorites include Peking duck with caviar and Grilled Wagyu beef with king soy sauce. Also available is a dim sum menu. Award-winning wine list and menu of signature cocktails.

THE HAVELOCK TAVERN

57 Masbro Rd, London, +44 20 7603 5374
www.havelocktavern.com
CUISINE: Pizza, Mediterranean
DRINKS: Beer & Wine Only
SERVING: Dinner; closed Mondays
PRICE RANGE: $$
NEIGHBORHOOD: West Kensington
Visit this very reasonably priced gastropub serving an international menu of delicious dishes including duck, fish and (really good) steaks if you want to avoid the really pricey nearby eateries in Notting Hill and Kensington. Menu changes daily. Good ales, cider and draft beers.

HAWKSMOOR SPITALFIELDS

157 Commercial St, London, +44 20 7426 4850
www.thehawksmoor.com
CUISINE: Steakhouse
DRINKS: Full Bar
SERVING: Lunch, Dinner
PRICE RANGE: $$$$
NEIGHBORHOOD: Spitalfields
This is the place if you're a steak lover. This steakhouse serves dictionary-thick Longhorn steaks, the oldest purebred cattle in the U.K. Other menu favorites include Grilled Free-Range Chicken and Native Grilled Lobster. For dessert there's a selection of puddings and, of course, after dinner drinks.

HÉLÈNE DARROZE AT THE CONNAUGHT

Carlos Place, Mayfair, 020-3147-7200.
www.the-connaught.co.uk/restaurants-bars/helene-darroze-at-the-connaught
CUISINE: French - Haute
DRINKS: Full Bar
SERVING: Lunch, Dinner
PRICE RANGE: $$$$
NEIGHBORHOOD: Mayfair
This is one of Mayfair's most elegant and posh Michelin dining experiences, with its blond-stained wooden paneling giving the room a more casual feel as you gaze through the windows toward the leafy trees in the square across the street. This eatery serves exquisite upscale French cuisine using the best ingredients money can buy. (They buy the ingredients first, and you buy them second, with a hefty mark-up.) The duck comes from France. The lobster from Cornwall. You get the idea. If you can't get a good meal here, you're *very* hard to please. Comprehensive wine list. Reservations recommended. You can't actually go wrong eating anywhere in the Connaught. Don't forget that **Jean-Georges** has a big presence here with his eponymous dining room. He not only has his signature named restaurant here, with its floor-to-ceiling windows offering a beautiful view of the square, but he runs the famous **Connaught Grill** as well. I can't stand what they've done with the old Grill. They've stripped it down to the point that it looks like a tarted-up version of a Hungry Sizzler steak house in some backwater town in Mississippi. Very sad. It's almost worth just getting a

bite at one of the intimate bars here. There's the **Connaught Bar** and the **Coburg Bar,** both of which are very clubby, dark, intimate and nice. They each have small plate menus that will do you very nicely. Like all the great hotels in the world, it's not in the least important where you eat in any of them. It's only important that you experience the wonder of some of these grand pleasure palaces. And you can do that for the price of a cocktail expertly prepared. There's also a very fine **Afternoon Tea** in the Connaught. You certainly don't want to pass through London without indulging in Afternoon Tea. The English do it better than anybody else.

HEREFORD ROAD
3 Hereford Rd, Westbourne Grove, London, +44 20 7727 1144
www.herefordroad.org
CUISINE: British cuisine
DRINKS: Full Bar
SERVING: Lunch, Dinner
PRICE RANGE: $$$$
NEIGHBORHOOD: Notting Hill
Just above the Bayswater Road is this elegant restaurant with an excellent menu of fresh English cuisine. Chef Tom Pemberton takes food preparation seriously and customers get to see most of the work in the open kitchen. Menu favorites include Deviled duck livers and Lamb Rump with purple sprouting broccoli; roasted quail with aioli; braised cuttlefish; cold roasted duck breast with pickled chicory, artichokes and roasted shallots;

whole braised lamb's neck (I know it sounds awful, but it's delicious). A no-frills but delightful experience.

HIDE
85 Piccadilly, Mayfair, 020-3146-8666
http://hide.co.uk
CUISINE: European (Modern)
DRINKS: Full Bar
SERVING: Breakfast, Lunch, Dinner
PRICE RANGE: $$$$
NEIGHBORHOOD: Mayfair
This is a modern three-level restaurant offering a fun and elegant dining experience. Very sleek, very modern, very industrial, dramatic lighting, a bustling crowd, lots of fun. You forget how stiff and stuffy those other Michelin-starred restaurants can be when you pop into a place like this throwing off an electric vibe, thrumming with excitement and vitality. High above Piccadilly, you can get a good view of Green Park. This place is just as good for any meal, breakfast, lunch or dinner. Menu picks: Roasted Scallops and Roasted Herdwick Lamb with Smoked

Cockles. I'd never had a smoked cockle before, but I did here. Incredible wine selection and the prices aren't as devastating as a lot of other places working at this level of sophistication. The entire place seems to be made of wood. Late night dining. Lunch is a la carte, dinner is tasting menus only. Reservations recommended.

IMAD'S SYRIAN KITCHEN

Top Floor, Kingly Court, Carnaby St, London, +44 20 7434 2448
https://www.imadssyriankitchen.co.uk
CUISINE: Middle Eastern
DRINKS: Full Bar
SERVING: Lunch, Dinner, Brunch
PRICE RANGE: $$$
NEIGHBORHOOD: Piccadilly Circus
Upscale Middle Eastern eatery in a bright and uplifting room. Favorites: Jaj Barghol (Grilled chicken thigh, bulgur wheat, savory spices); Fattet Macdous (Minced lamb, baby aubergine, tahini—my favorite dish here); and the Falafel. Creative desserts like Syrian ice cream with pistachio and candy floss. Reservations required.

THE IVY
1-5 West St, London, +44 20 7836 4751
www.the-ivy.co.uk/
CUISINE: Modern European
DRINKS: Full Bar
SERVING: Lunch, Dinner
PRICE RANGE: $$$
NEIGHBORHOOD: Covent Garden
This old school restaurant offers a simple menu of really good food. This well-known eatery is a favorite of celebrities and politicians-even at lunch. Menu favorites include Bang-bang chicken and Herb-roasted salmon. Dessert selection includes Crème Brule and Chocolate Fondant. Impressive wine list. Upstairs there's a private members' club. Reservations recommended.

JOSE
194 Bermondsey St, London, +44 020 7378 9455
www.josepizarro.com
CUISINE: Spanish, Tapas Bars
DRINKS: Beer & Wine Only
SERVING: Lunch, Dinner
PRICE RANGE: $$
NEIGHBORHOOD: Borough
This is a standing room-only in this very bustling joint that serves authentic Spanish tapas like prawns *a la plancha*. Menu favorites include tomato bread, pimentos de Padron, chorizo, Iberico pork cheek, hake, and mixed cheeses. Nice wine offerings. Menu changes daily.

KILN
58 Brewer St, London, **No Phone**
www.kilnsoho.com
CUISINE: Thai
DRINKS: Full Bar
SERVING: Lunch & Dinner; Closed Saturdays
PRICE RANGE: $$
NEIGHBORHOOD: Soho
Casual eatery with an open kitchen serving noodles & Thai-inspired dishes (a lot of them very spicy, wow!). Try to sit at the counter, even if it involves a wait. Much more exciting experience. Favorites: Aged Lamb & Cumin Skewer; Fried monkfish; Clay Pot Baked Glass Noodles. No reservations unless you're in a group.

KITTY FISHER'S WOOD GRILL
arket, London, +44 20 3302 1661
rs.com
ish cuisine
Bar

SERVING: Lunch & Dinner; Dinner only on Saturdays; closed Sundays
PRICE RANGE: $$$$
NEIGHBORHOOD: Mayfair
Dimly lit small eatery in historic Shepherd Market that seats about 40 people in an elegant setting that will leave no doubt you're in Mayfair, with its gold-framed art pieces, red banquettes, elaborate sconces. Menu is modern British fare with a Spanish twist. Favorites: Cornish crab with BBQ'd cucumber and Whipped cod roe on bread. Good cocktail and wine menu.

KOL

9 Seymour St, London, +44 20 3829 6888
https://kolrestaurant.com
CUISINE: Mexican
DRINKS: Full Bar
SERVING: Lunch & Dinner
PRICE RANGE: $$$$
NEIGHBORHOOD: Bond Street
Hip eatery offering a menu of Mexican-British fusion cuisine. The challenge here is that they make Mexican food using lots of British ingredients, often with wonderful results. Set menus with 7 or 9 courses. Favorites: Octopus Tiradito and Carnitas. Reservations required.

KRICKET

12 Denman St, Soho, London, +44 20 3019 8120
www.kricket.co.uk
CUISINE: Indian / Anglo-Indian
DRINKS: Full Bar (with great specialty cocktails)
SERVING: Lunch & Dinner; Closed Sundays
PRICE RANGE: $$
NEIGHBORHOOD: Soho
Funky joint serving Indian-inspired small plates. On the first floor they welcome walk-in traffic, while below in the basement there is service at communal tables with reservations. The only problem with that is it's more exciting upstairs at the bar. I advise going a little earlier and taking your chance for a seat or wait for one. Favorites: Tandoori grouse; Keralan fried chicken (very flavorful & spicy); and Coorgi Pork Cheek. Reservations recommended.

LA BODEGA NEGRA

16 Moor St, London, +44 20 4580 1186
www.labodeganegra.com
CUISINE: Mexican
DRINKS: Full Bar
SERVING: Lunch, Dinner, closed Mondays
PRICE RANGE: $$$
NEIGHBORHOOD: Bloomsbury
Guests enter through a faux sex shop front like an old speakeasy
of the 1930s. The place has a buzz and you feel like you've just
entered a party. Of course, the margaritas are plentiful and the
menu is typical Mexican fare. Menu favorites include Seafood
cazuela (similar to paella) and Lamb shank. The experience may
surpass the cuisine but it's a fun visit.

LA FAMIGLIA

7 Langton St, The World's End, London, +44 20 7351 0761
www.lafamiglia.co.uk
CUISINE: Italian, Gluten-Free
DRINKS: Beer & Wine
SERVING: Lunch, Dinner, closed Mondays
PRICE RANGE: $$$
NEIGHBORHOOD: Chelsea
This well-known eatery serves authentic Italian cuisine. Menu
favorites include Lobster pasta and Fried battered mozzarella.

Delicious bread and bread sticks. Also, a great place for Sunday brunch. Reservations recommended.

LA GAVROCHE

43 Upper Brook St, London, +44 20 7408 0881
www.le-gavroche.co.uk
CUISINE: French
DRINKS: Full Bar
SERVING: Lunch, Dinner, closed Sun & Mon
PRICE RANGE: $$$$
NEIGHBORHOOD: Marylebone
This fine-dining establishment offers top-notch classical French cuisine from Michel Roux, Jr. Here you'll find their justifiably famous cheese soufflé along with hot foie gras on a crisp duck pancake with cinnamon. Menu favorites include the Loin of Venison with walnut gnocchi. Desserts include apricot and Cointreau soufflés, which will melt in your mouth. The wine list is excellent with a selection of top French wines.

THE LEDBURY

127 Ledbury Rd, London, +44 20 7792 9090
www.theledbury.com
CUISINE: Modern European
DRINKS: Full Bar
SERVING: Lunch, Dinner, closed Sun & Mon
PRICE RANGE: $$$$

NEIGHBORHOOD: Notting Hill
This trendy spot offers a savory menu with delights such as Loin
and Shoulder of lamb and Roast Sea Bass. Desserts are just as
tasty with choices like: Passion Fruit Soufflé with Sauternes Ice
Cream and Banana and Chocolate Malt Tartlet. If you can book
a table it's a pleasing experience.

LE MANOIR AUX QUAF'SAISONS
Church Rd, Great Milton, Oxford, +44 1844 278881
www.manoir.com
CUISINE: French
DRINKS: Full Bar
SERVING: Lunch, Dinner
PRICE RANGE: $$$$
NEIGHBORHOOD: London Bridge
A favorite of foodies, this eatery is for those with a passion for
food. The chefs use the freshest and best quality ingredients,
most from their two-acre garden. Try the 6-course tasting menu
for a nice variety. Menu favorites include the Summer Vegetable
Risotto. Their wine cellar boasts approximately 1,000

different wines from around the world. An experience you won't
forget. Reservations necessary.

LOCANDA LOCATELLI

8 Seymour St, Marylebone, 020-7935 9088
www.locandalocatelli.com
CUISINE: Italian
DRINKS: Full Bar
SERVING: Lunch, Dinner
PRICE RANGE: $$$$
NEIGHBORHOOD: Marylebone
Elegant eatery serving classic Italian fare with a twist in a nice location next to the Churchill Hotel in an elegant room with modern decor. A very lively crowd comes to this Michelin-starred place, which is without question one of the best Italian restaurants in all London. Favorites: Linguine with Cornish Lobster and Sliced cured pork belly. Extensive wine list. Reservations recommended.

LYLE'S
Tea Building

56 Shoreditch High St, London, +44 20 3011 5911
www.lyleslondon.com
CUISINE: British

DRINKS: Full Bar
SERVING: Breakfast, Lunch & Dinner; closed Sundays
PRICE RANGE: $$$
NEIGHBORHOOD: Shoreditch
Simple industrial-style eatery offering a menu of seasonal British fare. The set menu changes daily, depending on what the chef wants to cook, and his decision is made based on what he's able to get from his specially selected suppliers. The chef says, "I think of it as commonsense cooking, buying from good fishermen, good farms, from people of similar mindset, just sensible, not reinventing the wheel." Warning: don't stuff yourself with the plentiful delicious sourdough bread. Twice I've ruined my dinner gobbling down too much of this delicious bread. Favorites: Lamb Sweetbreads and Mutton tartare. Try the Caramel Ice Cream for dessert. The wine list here is nicely affordable.

MAMBOW
78 Lower Clapton Rd, London. +020 3928 1000
www.mambow.co.uk/
CUISINE: Malaysian
DRINKS: Wine & Beer
SERVING: Lunch, Dinner
PRICE RANGE: $$
NEIGHBORHOOD: Lower Clapton
Located in the Market Peckham, this laid-back new eatery offering modern Malaysian cuisine. Open kitchen with bar seating, a few small tables, and customers order at the bar. Favorites include Black Pepper Curry Chicken and the Lor Bak (five-spice pork and prawn bean curd roll). Creative desserts worth trying.

MARU

18 Shepherd Market, London, +44 20 3637 7677
https://www.marulondon.com
CUISINE: Japanese
DRINKS: Wine & Sake
SERVING: Lunch & Dinner
PRICE RANGE: $$$
NEIGHBORHOOD: Mayfair
A 20-course Omakase upscale Japanese eatery using UK
ingredients with a strong focus on dry-ageing fish, tuna, brill,
trout, and squid. It's a long & somewhat boring evening, but the
food's delicious. Impressive sake selection. 10-seat counter
experience. Reservations only.

MILK

18-20 Bedford Hill, London, +44 4420 8772 9085
https://milklondonshop.uk/
CUISINE: British
DRINKS: Full Bar
SERVING: Breakfast, Lunch & Dinner; closed Sundays
PRICE RANGE: $$$
NEIGHBORHOOD: Balham
Popular local daytime café known for its specialty coffees and
innovative cuisine. The atmosphere is very cozy, homey, like an

old farmhouse, with simple wooden tables, old wallpaper. Everything is made from scratch, so you'll love it as much as I did. Favorites: Crumpets with goat's curd and honey and "Young Betty" (poached eggs with bacon and hollandaise on sourdough). Outdoor seating.

MIMI MEI FAIR
55 Curzon St, London, + 020 3989 7777
https://mimimeifair.com
CUISINE: Chinese
DRINKS: Wine
SERVING: Lunch & Dinner
PRICE RANGE: $$$
NEIGHBORHOOD: Mayfair
Upscale Chinese eatery (set in an old Georgian townhouse near Green Park) featuring a six-course tasting menu and a la carte menu in an incredibly elegant atmosphere. Favorites: the whole Peking Duck is the star here, carved gently at the table so you can make your little pancakes; the Golden Langoustine with black Périgord truffle is a standout. Wine selection includes over 200 labels.

MONOCLE CAFÉ
18 Chiltern St, London, +44 20 7135 2040
www.monocle.com/about/contacts/london-cafe
CUISINE: Coffee & Tea
DRINKS: Beer & Wine
SERVING: Sweets & Baked goods
PRICE RANGE: $$
NEIGHBORHOOD: Marylebone
Great place for coffee and sweets like pastries and baked goods from Stockholm's Fabrique bakery. Other offerings include Japanese chocolate bars and rollcake.

NEPTUNE
Principal Hotel
Corner Guilford St & Russell Sq, London, + 020 7520 1806
www.neptune.london
CUISINE: Seafood
DRINKS: Full Bar
SERVING: Lunch & Dinner Mon – Fri; Dinner only Sat & Sun
PRICE RANGE: $$$$
NEIGHBORHOOD: Bloomsbury
Modern seafood-focused eatery with an oyster bar. Extensive menu. Favorites: White Lobster, Wild mussels with saffron, bay leaf and orange sofritto; Rump steak. Elegant dining. Wine list mostly French.

Ottolenghi

OTTOLENGHI

287 Upper St, London, +44 20 7288 1454
www.ottolenghi.co.uk
CUISINE: Mediterranean
DRINKS: Beer & Wine Only
SERVING: Breakfast, Lunch, & Dinner
PRICE RANGE: $$
NEIGHBORHOOD: Islington

Both a restaurant and a deli, this happening place is designed so that it looks and feels like a retail store that ought to be selling high fashion. Instead, it's a restaurant with salads on the counter that change daily. Try to come in the evening when they bring out the candles and the place becomes more sophisticated. Weekend brunch is too crowded, so come during a weekday. Don't overlook the delectable, jarred items you can buy in the deli. Favorites: Roasted Aubergine (eggplant) and Burrata with butternut squash. Breakfast—get the Dutch baby pancake with poached fruit. Communal dining. Reservations for dinner only. Popular pre-theatre destination.

Ottolenghi

PADELLA

6 Southwark St, London, **no phone**
www.padella.co
CUISINE: Italian
DRINKS: Beer & Wine Only
SERVING: Lunch & Dinner; no reservations
PRICE RANGE: $$
NEIGHBORHOOD: London Bridge

Modern bistro with a small menu of Italian cuisine. This place is lots of fun. If you go for lunch, you'll have to wait in a line, but if you go for dinner, you put your name in and they will text you when the table's ready. Meantime, you go to one of the many nearby pubs in Borough-Market and have a drink. Opt for the upstairs, which is busier at the counters where you can watch the cooks hand-rolling pasta. Downstairs is a more intimate, so decide on your mood. For the quality of the pasta here, the prices are very affordable. So a lot of locals frequent the place. (To be honest, the portions are a little on the small side, so order a third dish—it's cheap enough.) Favorites: Pappardelle with the beef-shin ragu (their specialty); and Gnocchi with nutmeg butter. Nice wine list. No reservations, you need to show up 30-45 minutes before the restaurant opens at 5 p.m. Very busy. You can add your name to the queue on their website.

PALOMAR
34 Rupert St, London, +44 20 7439 8777
www.thepalomar.co.uk
CUISINE: Middle Eastern/Mediterranean
DRINKS: Full Bar
SERVING: Lunch & Dinner
PRICE RANGE: $$$
NEIGHBORHOOD: Soho
Unique eatery offering Modern fare from Jerusalem with an international twist. The kubaneh and tzatziki were amazing. But here it's really about the excitement level created by a smart staff and hip diners. Favorites: Octo-hummus and Beetroot carpaccio. Open kitchen so you can watch the food being prepared.

PIDGIN
52 Wilton Way, London, +44 20 7254 8311
www.pidginlondon.com
CUISINE: British (but Asian inspired)
DRINKS: Full Bar
SERVING: Dinner, Lunch & Dinner on Sat & Sun
PRICE RANGE: $$$
NEIGHBORHOOD: Hackney
Small simple eatery offering Asian-inspired/European cuisine that's impossible to categorize. They serve the same 4-course set menu for lunch and dinner, with the menu changing every week. (The pride themselves on not repeating a dish for over a year.) Example of a recent menu at press time: Haddock with wonton; sourdough, brown butter; Scallop, clam, land cress & black currant; Pork with sweet potato & oregano; Duck, grelot, cocoa nib; a couple of interesting desserts. Whatever they concoct, you'll love it. Trust me. Never been disappointed here, ever. Quite romantic at night. Nice wine list.

PIZARRO

194 Bermondsey St, London, +44 20 7378 9455
https://josepizarro.com/venues/pizarro-restaurant-bermondsey/
CUISINE: Spanish
DRINKS: Full Bar
SERVING: Lunch & Dinner
PRICE RANGE: $$
NEIGHBORHOOD: Borough
Large modern restaurant fitted out like a warehouse, with its brick walls, large, planked floors, old chandeliers and fixtures. They serve tapas and contemporary Spanish fare. Set menu with a variety of starters. Favorites: sweetbreads with mustard and mayo and girolle mushrooms with Manchego & truffle oil.

PIZZERIA MOZZA
TREEHOUSE HOTEL

14-15 Langham Pl, London, + 0800 917 1141
https://www.treehousehotels.com/london/eat-drink/pizzeria-mozza
CUISINE: Pizza
DRINKS: Full Bar
SERVING: Lunch & Dinner, Weekend Brunch
PRICE RANGE: $$
NEIGHBORHOOD: Marylebone

First established in Los Angeles, this is the first UK Pizza
Mozza. Menu features signature pizzas with a variety of
toppings including everything from fried capers, red onion, and
anchovies. You might even come away from your meal here
with the idea that this is the way forward in the world of pizza.
Unlike anything you've had before. Lots of Italian-inspired side
snacks and salads. Specials like Meatless Mondays and Fish
Fridays. Organic wines and classic Italian cocktails.

POLLEN STREET SOCIAL
8/10 Pollen St, London, +44 20 7290 7600
www.pollenstreetsocial.com
CUISINE: British
DRINKS: Full Bar
SERVING: Lunch, Dinner
PRICE RANGE: $$$$
NEIGHBORHOOD: Marylebone
Chef Jason Atherton of Ramsay's Maze offers a casual dining
menu that includes eight starters and eight mains. Menu
favorites include Roasted Atlantic Halibut and Lake District rack
of lamb. Vegetarian selections available. Desserts feature the
signature "PBJ" – a peanut parfait and Goat's milk rice pudding
with goat's cheese ice-cream. The wine list is quite large and
there's also a nice selection of lagers.

THE PORTRAIT BY RICHARD CORRIGAN
2 St. Martin's Place, London, +44 20 38727610
https://theportraitrestaurant.com/
CUISINE: British
DRINKS: Full Bar
SERVING: All Day (Gallery hours)
PRICE RANGE: $$$
NEIGHBORHOOD: Trafalgar Square
When visiting The National Gallery, may I suggest The Portrait
by Richard Corrigan. A friendly but upscale casual eatery on the
fourth floor of the Gallery. My favorite was the Halibut main,
served with a bright green spinach puree. For meat eaters they
serve tender lamb chops. Creative desserts that I lost the battle to
refuse (I had the macaron). Nice wine selection but their
cocktails like the chilli pepper margarita are very tempting.

THE PRINCE ARTHUR
95 Forest Rd, London, +44 20 7249 1119
www.theprincearthure8.com/
CUISINE: Gastropubs
DRINKS: Full Bar
SERVING: Bar menu with Sunday Roasts
PRICE RANGE: $$
NEIGHBORHOOD: Dalston
Neighborhood pub with tasty menu of small and large plate
dishes like Haddock & chips and Lobster bisque and scallops.
Great for meeting friends or a laid-back dinner. The lobster
bisque was my favorite. Creative wine list, citrusy cocktails, and
well-pour Guinness.

QUO VADIS

26-29 Dean St, London, +44 20 7437 9585
www.quovadissoho.co.uk
CUISINE: Seafood
DRINKS: Full Bar
SERVING: Lunch, Dinner
PRICE RANGE: $$$
NEIGHBORHOOD: Soho
Open since 1926, this charming little restaurant serves primarily modern British cuisine. Menu changes daily. Menu favorites include Shepherd's Pie and Breast of Lamb. Pre-theatre menu for the theatre crowd. Nice cocktails. Private club upstairs.

RANDALL & AUBIN

14- 16 Brewer St, London, +44 20 7287 4447
www.randallandaubin.com
CUISINE: Seafood/British
DRINKS: Full Bar
SERVING: Lunch, Dinner
PRICE RANGE: $$$
NEIGHBORHOOD: Soho
This hip eatery is a great choice for a date or hanging with friends. Here you'll find an excellent choice of seafood and French and English dishes. Nice wine list. Menu favorites

include Seafood platter (enough for two) and Rotisserie chicken. Extensive wine list.

RESTAURANT STORY
199 Tooley St, London, +44 20 7183 2117
www.restaurantstory.co.uk
CUISINE: Pizza, Mediterranean
DRINKS: Beer & Wine Only
SERVING: Lunch & Dinner; closed Sunday & Monday
PRICE RANGE: $$$$
NEIGHBORHOOD: London Bridge; Bermondsey
Just on the south bank of the Thames in a high-ceilinged room with floor to ceiling glass windows that give it an open, airy feel is this this Michelin-starred eatery where you can choose between two menus – 6 or 10 courses. All courses come with delicious warm homemade bread. Favorites: Scallops, cucumber and dill ash and Beef tartare, apple and Perigord truffle. Truly an unforgettable dining experience.

THE RIDING HOUSE CAFÉ
43-51 Great Titchfield St, London, +44 20 7927 0840
www.riding.house/
CUISINE: British/Tapas
DRINKS: Full Bar
SERVING: Brunch, Lunch, Dinner
PRICE RANGE: $$
NEIGHBORHOOD: Fitzrovia
This hipster chic brasserie attracts a variety of crowds depending on the time of day you may be seated next to film execs or media brass. Dinner menu favorites include Lobster lasagna and Venison Haunch. Known for their signature cocktails and impressive wine list. Dessert choices include Baked Alaska and Sticky Toffee Pudding.

Restaurant Terrace, The Ritz

THE RITZ RESTAURANT
150 Piccadilly, 020-7300 2370/ +44 20 7493 8181
www.theritzlondon.com/dine-with-us/the-ritz-restaurant
CUISINE: European (Modern) / British
DRINKS: Full Bar
SERVING: Breakfast, Lunch, Dinner
PRICE RANGE: $$$$
NEIGHBORHOOD: St James's
Visiting the Ritz is like going to Buckingham Palace or the British Museum. It's a quintessential English thing to do. I could say the same thing about Claridge's or Brown's hotel or any number of other places, but the Ritz always stands out. The elegant marble columns and sumptuous décor of its public rooms, the fine quality of its restaurant and bar offerings—it's all very hard to beat. If the weather's good, try hard to get a table out on the **Restaurant Terrace at the Ritz**. The lovely flower boxes are bursting with color and you'll get a view of Green Park from up here. There's another little gem called the **Secret Garden Bar**, but the Terrace is more memorable. You'll never forget those flower boxes. The main dining room at the Ritz is not fun. It's gorgeous, don't get me wrong. Just so stuffy and formal. You'll feel like you're dining in an aristocrat's house, but that he doesn't really want you there as a guest. Take a peek in just to see what it looks like but eat in one of the other rooms. Overall, this is an upscale eatery in a baroque setting serving

British/French cuisine. Menu picks: Loin of Venison with smoked parsnip and the classic Beef Wellington. (I love parsnips, but a lot of people don't.) There's **Afternoon Tea**, of course, one of the best in town. And don't overlook the charming intimate dark bars here at the Ritz. It's not the Paris Ritz, but it's close enough.

Main dining room, The Ritz

ROVI

59 Wells St, London, +44 20 3963 8270
https://ottolenghi.co.uk/restaurants/rovi
CUISINE: Mediterranean
DRINKS: Full Bar
SERVING: Lunch & Dinner; Dinner only Mon – Wed, Lunch only on Sunday
PRICE RANGE: $$$
NEIGHBORHOOD: Fitzrovia

Upscale 85-seat eatery with tables ranged around an elegant horseshow-shaped bar in the center of the room with highlights of marble and unfinished blond oak. The menu focuses on vegetables, but there are plenty of meat options. Favorites: Crumpet lobster toast; Grilled Octopus and Beef Carpaccio. The Jerusalem mixed grill features chicken thighs roasted over flames and they are so good I got this dish on my second visit. Very clever and surprising menu twists. Creative cocktails.

SABOR
35-37 Heddon St, London +44 20 3319 8130
https://www.saborrestaurants.co.uk/
CUISINE: Mediterranean / European / Spanish
DRINKS: Full Bar
SERVING: Lunch & Dinner
PRICE RANGE: $$$$
NEIGHBORHOOD: Mayfair
Upscale eatery focusing on the flavors of Spain reminiscent of
the Spanish tapas bars. Favorite dishes: Paella and Cuttlefish.
Impressive wine list featuring mostly Spanish labels.
Reservations recommended.

SCOTT'S
20 Mount St, London, +44 20 7495 7309
www.scotts-restaurant.com
CUISINE: Seafood, British
DRINKS: Full Bar
SERVING: Lunch, Dinner
PRICE RANGE: $$$$

NEIGHBORHOOD: Mayfair
This is one of London's great fish restaurants from the people
who own the Ivy and Le Caprice. Here you'll find great seafood
and a grand oyster bar as the restaurant's centerpiece. Menu
favorites include Bass ceviche and Halibut Fillet. Check out the
champagne and oyster bar. Here you'll find an impressive
cocktail menu and wine list that complements the varied menu.
Save room for the delicious desserts like the Bakewell pudding.

SEXY FISH
@ BERKELEY SQUARE HOUSE
4-6 Berkeley Sq, London, +44 20 3764 2000
www.sexyfish.com
CUISINE: Japanese/Asian Fusion
DRINKS: Full Bar
SERVING: Lunch & Dinner
PRICE RANGE: $$$$
NEIGHBORHOOD: Mayfair
Upscale, art-filled eatery focusing primarily on Asian fish and
shellfish. Worth coming here for the wonderful design—there
are floating fish lamps designed by Frank Gehry, hand cut
collage art adorning the ceiling designed by Michael Roberts,
bronze mermaids cast by Damien Hirst, unusual lightning
fixtures. The bar here is spectacular. Favorites: Miso Chilean sea

bass and Yellowtail with smoked tofu and caviar. Creative desserts like warm out of the over cinnamon donuts.

SIX BY NICO
41 Charlotte St, London, +44 20 7580 8143
www.sixbynico.co.uk/
CUISINE: Italian/Fusion
DRINKS: Full Bar
SERVING: Lunch & Dinner
PRICE RANGE: $$$
NEIGHBORHOOD: Fitzrovia
Upscale eatery in an industrial setting with parquet brickwork, brushed copper, those lighting fixtures that scream out for little shades. They offer tasting menus with wine pairings. The "Six" in the name refers to the 6-course tasting menu. And to the idea that every 6 weeks, the menu changes, reflecting a new theme. Prices are much lower than most "tasting menus" you find in town, another plus in this fast, fun and friendly place. Menu

picks: Fish Fingers (Salmon Tartare/Kohlrabi) and Truffle Mac
'N Cheese. Reservations.

SOIF
27 Battersea Rise, London, +44 20 7223 1112
www.soif.co
CUISINE: British
DRINKS: Full Bar
SERVING: Breakfast, Lunch & Dinner; closed Sundays
PRICE RANGE: $$$
NEIGHBORHOOD: Clapham Common, Clapham Junction
Cute little eatery serving up a combination of British and French
fare – mostly small plates. Menu picks: Beef tartare and Quail
with harissa and yogurt. Impressive wine list – mostly French
labels.

SMOKEHOUSE
63-69 Canonbury Rd, London, +44 20 7354 1144
www.smokehouseislington.co.uk
CUISINE: Smokehouse
DRINKS: Full Bar
SERVING: Dinner, Lunch on Sat & Sun
PRICE RANGE: $$$
NEIGHBORHOOD: Canonbury, Islington
Upscale smokehouse offering a small a-la carte menu of smoked
and grilled food. Favorites: Short-rib bourguignon and any of the
steaks. 20 craft beers on tap and 40 in a bottle. Wine list of small
family producers only.

SPRING

Somerset House
New Wing Lancaster Place, London, + 44 20 3011 0115
www.springrestaurant.co.uk
CUISINE: Modern European / British
DRINKS: Lunch, Dinner, & Brunch
SERVING: Lunch & Dinner
PRICE RANGE: $$$$
NEIGHBORHOOD: Strand
Located inside the new wing of the Somerset House, this upscale
eatery offers a creative menu of European fare. The atmosphere
is cool, calm, collected. Lots of white is used in the décor, giving
the place a bright, cherry feeling, but also a lot of formality. The
peach-colored chairs offer a little break from the cool white
interior. (I think they're peach—I am a little bit color-blind in
that shade.) At night the place is transformed into an utterly
elegant, romantic room, with soft lighting that even flattered me.
Favorites: Wild halibut with roasted endive and Filet of beef.
Curated wine list.

ST JOHN

26 St John St, London, +44 20 7251 0848
https://stjohnrestaurant.com/
CUISINE: British

DRINKS: Full Bar
SERVING: Lunch, Dinner
PRICE RANGE: $$$
NEIGHBORHOOD: Farringdon
This place is for meat lovers and the mezzanine dining room is in the former Smithfield smokehouse. Menu favorites include Bone Marrow and Grouse and Deviled kidneys. Wine list of all French wines.

SWEETINGS FISH RESTAURANT
39 Queen Victoria St, London, +44 20 7248 3062
https://www.sweetingsrestaurant.com/
CUISINE: British
DRINKS: No Booze
SERVING: Lunch only
PRICE RANGE: $$$
NEIGHBORHOOD: The City
First opened in 1889, this restaurant now offers a wide variety of sustainable fish. Menu favorites include: the classic Fish Pie might be the best of its kind in all London; Smoked Trout is good; the crab and smoked fish rolls will not disappoint. Nice wine list to complement fish dishes. Homemade puddings for dessert.

TERROIRS

5 William IV St, London, +44 20 7036 0660
www.terroirswinebar.com
CUISINE: French
DRINKS: Beer & Wine Only
SERVING: Lunch, Dinner
PRICE RANGE: $$
NEIGHBORHOOD: Covent Garden
This two-level wine bar and restaurant offers a selection of over 200 French and Italian wines but specializes in "natural wines." The menu offers a variety of simple dishes: charcuterie, tapas, and French-inspired dishes. Menu favorites include Blackened Shoulder of Lamb and Cod in Brown Shrimp Butter. Delicious dessert choices include Bitter Chocolate Pot Pudding and Yorkshire Rhubarb Pudding.

WATERHOUSE PROJECT

1 Corbridge Cres, London, +44 7841 804119
https://www.thewaterhouseproject.com
CUISINE: British
DRINKS: Full Bar
SERVING: Dinner: Fri & Sat only
PRICE RANGE: $$$$
NEIGHBORHOOD: Bethnal Green, East London, Hackney
Tickets must be purchased in advance for this dining experience.
Two communal tables (and some individual tables as well) and
supper club atmosphere. 9 tasting courses with paired wines.
The menu is kept secret until it's served, but you won't be

disappointed in anything this chef offers you because he was trained in a Michelin-starred restaurant not too far away.

WILTONS
55 Jermyn St, London, +44 20 7629 9955
www.wiltons.co.uk
CUISINE: Seafood
DRINKS: Full Bar
SERVING: Lunch, Dinner
PRICE RANGE: $$$$
NEIGHBORHOOD: Piccadilly
Established in 1742, this iconic restaurant continues serving great traditional English cuisine in an atmosphere that evokes the great private gentlemen's clubs of London. The menu is filled with items like wild fish (the Dover sole is exquisite), shellfish (Queen Victoria awarded them a Royal Warrant as purveyors of oysters to the Crown in 1884) and game in season. Menu favorites include Fillet of Cod and Sharphan park spelt risotto. Impressive wine list. Delicious desserts include the Morello cherry and chocolate soufflé. Seasonal menu.

THE WOLSELEY

160 Piccadilly, London, +44 20 7499 6996
www.thewolseley.com
CUISINE: Cafe
DRINKS: Full Bar
SERVING: Breakfast, Lunch, Dinner
PRICE RANGE: $$$
NEIGHBORHOOD: Mayfair

If you're one for impeccable service, this high-ceilinged Art Deco gem is the place. Here you'll get white-glove service in the grand European tradition. Known for its wonderful breakfast cuisine (get the very English "kedgeree," an Anglo-Indian inspired dish consisting of curried rice and smoked haddock with a poached egg served on top), the other menus are just as impressive. Menu favorites include Steak Tartare and Grilled Halibut. Great place for afternoon tea. Reservations recommended.

WRIGHT BROTHERS OYSTER & PORTER HOUSE

11 Stoney St, London, +44 20 7403 9554
www.thewrightbrothers.co.uk/
CUISINE: Seafood

DRINKS: Full Bar
SERVING: Lunch, Dinner
PRICE RANGE: $$$
NEIGHBORHOOD: London Bridge / Borough Market
This restaurant has a fast turnover and all the seating is high-backed stools. Menu changes daily and is written on a blackboard over the bar. If the weather permits, try to secure one of the big wooden barrels outside that serve as tables. Menu favorites include Oysters Japanese-style and Grilled Plaice. Great place for Sunday brunch with menu choices like smoked haddock kedgeree, and scrambled eggs with Hederman's organic smoked salmon. Nice wine list.

Chapter 5
<u>NIGHTLIFE</u>

214 BERMONDSEY
214 Bermondsey St, London, +44 20 7403 6875
www.two1four.com
NEIGHBORHOOD: Borough
Underneath the **Flour & Grape**, this small downstairs bar offers
a fun drinking experience. You'd never find this place unless
somebody like me alerted you to it. Brick walls, dim lighting,
lots of candles. If you're not into gin, this place may change
your mind. Great collection of gins but there are alternative
cocktails for non-gin drinkers.

BAR ITALIA

22 Frith St, Soho, London, +44 20 7734 4737
www.baritaliasoho.co.uk
NEIGHBORHOOD: Bloomsbury
This is a traditional 24-hour coffee bar where you can get
authentic Italian coffee, Portuguese custards, and panini
sandwiches. The barista behind the counter is genuine and so is
the coffee. Not a lounging sort of place but a 'get your espresso
and go' place. Also don't ask for complicated concoctions that
you might order at Starbucks.

BLIND PIG

58 Poland St, London, +44 20 7993 3251
www.socialeatinghouse.com
NEIGHBORHOOD: Soho
Great bar with character – something out of Harry Potter if he
was old enough to drink. This speakeasy style spot has a blind
with a blindfold on to welcome you. Excellent cocktails served
by bartenders who know their stuff. Small creative menu of bar
grub. Trendy types, media types, all types who love the
downstairs **Social Eating House** bistro located downstairs.

BLIND SPOT
St. Martins Hotel
Covent Garden, 45 St Martin's Ln, London, +44 20 7300 5588
https://book.ennismore.com/hotels/originals/st-martins-lane
NEIGHBORHOOD: Covent Garden
Chic and secret cocktail bar located in the luxury St. Martins
Hotel designed by Phillipe Starck featuring low lighting and
eclectic art. Great cocktails.

CADENHEAD'S WHISKEY SHOP & TASTING ROOM
26 Chiltern St, London, +44 20 7935 6999
https://www.cadenhead.scot/
NEIGHBORHOOD: Marylebone
This one-of-a-kind whiskey bottler offers spirits from distilleries
from all over Scotland and bottles them without filtration.
Chalkboards feature an extensive list of rare scotches, which are
available for sampling in the tasting room.

CAT & MUTTON
76 Broadway Market, London, +44 20 7249 6555
www.catandmutton.com
NEIGHBORHOOD: Broadway Market, London Fields
Traditional gastropub with a great selection of creative cocktails.
Bloody Marys and Bloody Caesars. Check out their Sunday

Roasts where they have great selection of food. Theme nights like Wednesday quiz night. Draws artists and sports fans.

CRAZY COQS

20 Sherwood St, London, +44 20 7734 4888
www.brasseriezedel.com/crazy-coqs
NEIGHBORHOOD: Soho
Jazz & Blues nightclub-cabaret. Intimate room for great performances. Check out the open mike night.

DUCK & WAFFLE

110 Bishopsgate, 40th Floor, London, +44 20 3640 7310
www.duckandwaffle.com
NEIGHBORHOOD: Aldgate
Upscale bar and eatery offering traditional British cuisine. Top-notch cocktails in a beautiful spot that welcomes guests 24/7. Dress code. Reservations necessary.

OPIUM

15-16 Gerrard St, London, +44 20 7734 7276
www.opiumchinatown.com
NEIGHBORHOOD: Chinatown
This place has the feel of an old speakeasy/opium den. There's a mixology school in the attic of this 3-story townhouse, and lots of the kids who go there come down here afterward to hang out.

Try the opium drink – it's light and sweet. Creative cocktails – tasty and strong.

THE PARLOUR AT MARYLEBONE ZETTER TOWNHOUSE

28-30 Seymour St, London, 020 7324 4544
www.thezettertownhouse.com
NEIGHBORHOOD: Marylebone
This is the intimate drawing room decorated with curious collections and antiques. Located in the Zetter Townhouse, a 24-bedroom Georgian townhouse, this unique cocktail lounge offers a unique cocktail experience. Private rooftop terrace.

THE PRINCE ARTHUR

95 Forest Rd, London, +44 20 7249 1119
www.theprincearthure8.com/
CUISINE: Gastropubs
DRINKS: Full Bar
SERVING: Bar menu with Sunday Roasts
PRICE RANGE: $$
NEIGHBORHOOD: Dalston
Neighborhood pub with tasty menu of small and large plate dishes like Haddock & chips and Lobster bisque and scallops. Great for meeting friends or a laid-back dinner. The lobster bisque was my favorite. Creative wine list, citrusy cocktails, and well-pour Guinness.

TERROIRS
5 William IV St, London, +44 20 7036 0660
www.terroirswinebar.com
NEIGHBORHOOD: Covent Garden, Strand
Cute little cozy French wine bar. If you get hungry they have a small menu of tapas-style plates and a couple of desserts. Huge selection of wines.

Chapter 6

WHAT TO SEE & DO

ABBA ARENA
1 Pudding Mill Ln, London
https://abbavoyage.com/thearena/
ABBA fans rejoice as you can now see the popular '70s group in concert once again almost live. With cutting-edge technology, the world can experience ABBA like they once looked with incredible musicians. The concert is 90 minutes long with no intermission. Doors open 1 hour 45 minutes before the start of the concert so you can enjoy the many bar and food outlets in the arena. Tickets available from £70.

AFTERNOON TEA

Don't have dinner one night and indulge one of London's most enjoyable traditions: afternoon tea. Among any number of places I'd recommend are: **Fortnum & Mason, Brown's, Claridge's** or **Langham.** You'll get your fill of sandwiches and scones and your sweet tooth will be sated with pastries. Plan your tea before taking in a play in the West End and you'll be able to get a snack afterwards.

ALMEIDA THEATER

Almeida St, London, +44 20 7359 4404
www.almeida.co.uk
NEIGHBORHOOD: Islington
Built in 1837, this theater opened in 1989 with a 325-seat studio theatre and has since gained an international reputation. Here you can see a diverse range of theatre including their annual summer festival of contemporary opera, music and theatre.

ASCOT PARK POLO ACADEMY

Windlesham Rd, Chobham, London, +44 1276 858545
www.polo.co.uk
NEIGHBORHOOD: Surrey
This is outside London in Surrey, but if you have the time, I'd
highly recommend traveling out to enjoy the 120 acres of
beautiful rural countryside near Windsor and Ascot where you'll
find this place. The Polo Club is the largest Polo Training
Academy in the world with a complete club facility for polo.
Here local and visiting international players and members play
polo in chukkas and matches. Polo instructors are available for
the novice. The Café Bar is open all weekends year-round.

BARCLAYS CYCLE HIRE

https://tfl.gov.uk/modes/cycling/santander-cycles
NEIGHBORHOOD: All over London
Biking is a great way to get around London. This system is great
as you can go to the nearest docking station with your debit or
credit card and rent a bike. You can return it to one of 720
stations located all over London. Trips under 30 minutes are
free.

BRITISH LIBRARY

96 Euston Rd, London NW1 2DB, +44 330 333 1144
www.bl.uk
NEIGHBORHOOD: Euston
This is the national library of the U.K. and a major research
library holding over 150 million items from many countries
including many languages and in many formats. The Library's
collection contains approximately 14 million books as well as
many manuscripts and historical items dating back to 2000 BC.
This is one of the two largest libraries in the world, second to the
Library of Congress in the U.S.

BRITISH MUSEUM

Great Russell St, London WC1B 3DG, +44 20 7323 8000
www.britishmuseum.org
NEIGHBORHOOD: Bloomsbury
ADMISSION: Free, tours daily
Established in 1753, the museum is dedicated to human history
and culture with a permanent collection of nearly 8 million
pieces. This is one of the largest and most comprehensive in
existence with work from all continents. The core of the building
was designed in the nineteenth century. Highlights of the
museum include the Round Reading Room with a domed ceiling
and the Great Court designed by Norman Foster. Exhibits

include History of the World in 100 Objects and permanent exhibitions from all over the world. The massive museum features an on-site restaurant, two cafes and a museum shop.

CHURCHILL WAR ROOMS
Clive Steps, King Charles St, London SW1A 2AQ, +44 20 7930 6961
www.iwm.org.uk
NEIGHBORHOOD: Westminster
ADMISSION: Modest Admission fee
A must-see for WWII aficionados, this museum, one of the five branches of the Imperial War Museum, holds a variety of treasures including the wartime bunker that sheltered Churchill during the Blitz. Here you can learn about the secret history of the underground. Also, home of the Churchill Museum that celebrates the life of Winston Churchill.

HMS BELFAST
The Queen's Walk, London SE1 2JH, +44 20 7940 6300
http://www.iwm.org.uk/
NEIGHBORHOOD: St Katherine Dock
ADMISSION: Minimal Admission fee
The HMS Belfast is a museum ship with nine decks open to the public. Part of Imperial War Museums, this unique museum shares the stories of life on board during World War II. Visitors can tour the nine decks that feature the heavily protected Shell Rooms to the Operations Room. Visitors can experience The Life at Sea exhibition, which shares stories from actual veterans and The Gun Turret Experience. Commissioned in1939 shortly before the outbreak of the Second World War, Belfast was initially part of the British naval blockade against Germany. Free audio guides available in English, French, German and Spanish.

LONDON FIELDS PARK
London Fields Westside, London, +44 20 8356 3000
www.hackney.gov.uk/london-fields
NEIGHBORHOOD: Hackney
London Fields Park is an impressive public park located in the north-east of Charing Cross. The park houses the only heated outdoor Olympic-size pool in London. The park also boasts a

cricket pitch, grass areas, a small BMX track, tennis courts, a table tennis table and two children's play areas. Here you find a favorite cycle path that runs from the Pub on the Park to Broadway Market. On Saturdays, there's an open-market with vendors selling everything from hot foods, handmade jewelry, gifts, fashions, and vintage clothing. On Sundays, there's a Farmers' Market and crafts market.

MUSEUMOF THE HOME
136 Kingsland Road, London E2 8EA, +44 20 7739 9893
http://www.geffrye-museum.org.uk
NEIGHBORHOOD: Hoxton
ADMISSION: Free, closed Mondays
This museum celebrates the history of the home and how homes and gardens reflect change. Here visitors can tour the series of period rooms that scan the centuries from 17th to 20th. The collections illustrate and exhibit furnishing from the past 400 years. The museum also features beautiful gardens.

MUSEUM OF LONDON
150 London Wall, London EC2Y 5HN, +44 20 7001 9844
www.museumoflondon.org.uk
NEIGHBORHOOD: Barbican
ADMISSION: Free

Located just north of St Paul's Cathedral on the edge of the oldest part of London, this museum documents London's history from prehistoric to modern times. The museum's galleries contain original artifacts, models, pictures and diagrams, archeological discoveries and interactive displays. Popular galleries include: "London Before London," the "Medieval London" gallery and "War, Plague and Fire."

MUSEUM OF LONDON DOCKLANDS
1 Warehouse, West India Quay, London E14 4AL, +44 20 7001 9844
www.museumoflondon.org.uk/docklands
NEIGHBORHOOD: Canary Wharf
ADMISSION: Free
Formerly the Museum in Docklands, this museum celebrates the history of London's River Thames and Docklands. The museum's collection features archives of the Port of London Authority and includes a large collection of historical artifacts, models, and pictures. The two level museum features 12 galleries and a children's gallery. The facility includes a lecture theater and meeting rooms that offer a schedule of talks and events. Also on-site is a reading room, a restaurant and a shop.

NATIONAL GALLERY
Trafalgar Square, London WC2N 5DN, +44 20 774 72885
www.nationalgallery.org.uk
NEIGHBORHOOD: Trafalgar Square
ADMISSION: Free
Founded in 1824, this art museum boasts a collection of over 2,300 works, dating from the mid-13th century to 1900. This is the fifth most visited art museum in the world. The current building was designed by William Wilkins and the Sainsbury Wing was designed by Robert Venturi and Denise Scott Brown.

NATURAL HISTORY MUSEUM

Cromwell Rd, London SW7 5BD, +44 20 7942 5000
www.nhm.ac.uk
NEIGHBORHOOD: South Kensington
ADMISSION: Free, there is a charge for some temporary
exhibitions
This museum features impressive natural history exhibitions and
is home to approximately 70 million pieces from five main
collections: botany, entomology, mineralogy, paleontology and
zoology. The museum is also a world-renowned research center
that specializes in taxonomy, identification and conservation.
The museum's collections contain great historical pieces
including specimens collected by Charles Darwin as well as
extensive books, journals, manuscripts, and artwork collections.

ST. JAMES CHURCH

197 Piccadilly, London, +44 20 7734 4511
www.sjp.org.uk
NEIGHBORHOOD: Piccadilly
The church known both as St James' Church, Piccadilly and St
James' Church, Westminster, opened in 1684 and was designed
and built by Sir Christopher Wren. The church was bombed and
destroyed in 1940 and not restored until 1954. The church
possesses celebrated reredos with carvings by Grinling Gibbons.

Today the church offers a variety of lectures and concerts. There is a small garden west of the tower.

ST PAUL'S CATHEDRAL

St Paul's Churchyard, London, +44 20 7246 8350
www.stpauls.co.uk
NEIGHBORHOOD: Blackfriars
ADMISSION: Nominal Admission fee
This Church of England cathedral, one of the most famous sights of London, is the seat of the Bishop of London. Sitting at the top of Ludgate Hill, this cathedral also acts as the mother church of the Diocese of London. Designed in the English Baroque style by Sir Christopher Wren, its construction was part of the major rebuilding program instigated after the Great Fire of London in 1666. Standing 365 feet high, the cathedral was the tallest building in London until 1962. Visitors can climb up the world-famous dome to the Whispering Gallery where a whisper can be heard clearly 100 feet away. View beautiful panoramic views of London by climbing 271 steps to the Golden Gallery located at the top of the dome.

TATE MODERN

Bankside, London SE1 9TG, +44 20 7887 8888
www.tate.org.uk/visit/tate-modern
NEIGHBORHOOD: Bankside
ADMISSION: Free except for special exhibitions
Britain's national gallery of international modern art is the most visited modern art gallery in the world. This museum holds Britain's national collection of art dating from 1500 to present day including international modern and contemporary art. The museum features works of some of the great artists including Andy Warhol, Marcel Duchamp, Salvador Dali, Henri Matisse, Pablo Picasso, Jackson Pollock and August Rodin. The main collection is exhibited in four wings – each taking up nearly half a floor. Tate Modern also features films, conferences and talks as well as a gift shop, café and restaurant.

TOWER OF LONDON

London EC3N 4AB, +44 20 3166 6000
www.hrp.org.uk/TowerOfLondon
NEIGHBORHOOD: Aldgate
ADMISSION: Moderate admission fee
This historic castle, also known as Her Majesty's Royal Palace and Fortress, is located on the north bank of the River Thames. Founded at the end of 1066 as part of the Norman Conquest of England, this castle was used as a prison from 1100 to 1952 and is one of London's most famous landmarks. Here you'll find the Crown Jewels, the prison cell of Sir Walter Raleigh and the Chapel of St. John and the Royal Armouries. The White Tower was built by William the Conqueror, where visitors can see exhibits from the Royal Armouries' collection. Visitors can join one of the famous Yeoman Warder tours to hear exciting tales of the Tower's past.

VICTORIA AND ALBERT MUSEUM

Cromwell Rd, London SW7 2RL, +44 20 7942 2000
www.vam.ac.uk
NEIGHBORHOOD: South Kensington
ADMISSION: Free

Founded in 1852 and named after Queen Victoria and Prince Albert, this is the world's largest museum of decorative arts and design. With a permanent collection of over 4.5 million objects, the museum covers 12.5 acres and 145 galleries. The exhibitions span over 5,000 years of art from cultures of Europe, North America, Asia and North Africa. Among the collection are ceramics, glass, textiles, costumes, silver, ironwork, furniture, jewelry, sculpture, medieval objects, drawings and photographs. The museum houses the world's largest collection of post-classical sculpture and the Western world's largest Islamic collection.

WALLACE COLLECTION
Hertford House, Manchester Square, London, +44 20 7563 9500
www.wallacecollection.org
NEIGHBORHOOD: Marylebone
ADMISSION: Free
This national museum (Hertford House) displays works of fine and decorative arts from the 15th to the 19th centuries. The collection also includes a large group of French 18th century paintings, furniture, arms & armor, porcelain and Old Master paintings exhibited in 25 galleries. The collection holds nearly 5,500 pieces and is probably best known for its eighteenth-century French paintings and French furniture.

WESTMINSTER ABBEY

20 Deans Yd, London SW1P 3PA, +44 20 7222 5152
www.westminster-abbey.org
NEIGHBORHOOD: Westminster
ADMISSION: Moderate admission fee

Formerly the Collegiate Church of St Peter at Westminster, the
Westminster Abbey is the one of the most notable religious
buildings in the U.K. The mostly Gothic structure has been the
burial place of British monarchs since 1245. An interesting sight
to visit is the Poet's Corner, located in the South Transept of the
Abbey, where poets such as Geoffrey Chaucer have been
honored here. Poets buried here include John Dryden, Alfred
Lord Tennyson, Robert Browning, and John Masefield and the
writers Samuel Johnson, Charles Dickens, Richard Brinsley
Sheridan, Rudyard Kipling, and Thomas Hardy. Another
highlight of the Abbey is the Jerusalem Chamber, a room that
was added in the 14th Century – this chamber was the meeting
place for the authors of the King James version of the Bible.
Visitors should also visit the three original gardens within the
Abbey: the Garth, the Little Cloister and College Garden as well
as St Catherine's Garden a newer garden.

Chapter 7
SHOPPING & SERVICES

11 BOUNDARY
11 Boundary St, London, +44 020 7033 0330
NEIGHBORHOOD: Shoreditch
Located in the heart of Shoreditch, this luxury fashion boutique offers an impressive collection of women's fashions, shoes, and jewelry including brands like Wildfox, By Malene Birger, and House of Harlow 1960.

BERRY BROS & RUDD
3 St James St, London, +44 800 280 2440
www.bbr.com
NEIGHBORHOOD: St James
As Britain's oldest wine and spirits merchant, Little has changed since the opening in 1698, Britain's oldest wine and spirits merchant, and you'll find an extensive collection of wines and spirits. You'll find everything from an assortment of Bordeaux to top Italian and New World classics.

DAUNT BOOKS
83 Marylebone High St, +44 20 7224 2295
www.dauntbooks.co.uk
NEIGHBORHOOD: Marylebone
An original Edwardian bookshop filled with beautiful long oak
galleries and skylights. This is a great source for travel
information for practically anyplace in the world. Here you'll
also find guidebooks, literary fiction, biography, gardening,
maps, history, politics and more.

LARGE GLASS
392 Caledonian Rd, London, +44 20 7609 9345
www.largeglass.co.uk
NEIGHBORHOOD: King's Cross
A beautiful art space/gallery, named after Duchamp's glass-
made image, that boasts pieces by Jacques Adnet, Jeff McMillan
and Richard Wentworth. The gallery also hosts tastings,
performances and film sessions.

LIBERTY DEPARTMENT STORE
Regent Street, London, +44 20 3893 3062
+44 20 3893 3062
www.liberty.co.uk
NEIGHBORHOOD: Soho

This iconic four-floor department store offers a wide range of luxury goods, fashions for men, women and children, cosmetics, fragrances, jewelry, housewares, furniture, and gifts. The Liberty Haberdashery department is on the third floor and boasts an impressive fabrics collection.

LOTS ROAD
71 Lots Rd, London, +44 20 7376 6800
www.lotsroad.com
NEIGHBORHOOD: West Brompton
This auction house offers a constantly changing collection of Contemporary and antique items. Here you'll find everything from silk rugs to handcrafted furniture. Auctions every Sundays starting at noon.

MOMOSAN SHOP
79a Wilton Way, London, +44 20 7249 4989
www.momosanshop.com
NEIGHBORHOOD: Shoreditch

This small shop features selected works from Japan as well as Europe and Scandinavia. Here you'll find interesting collections of art inspired products including kitchenware, lighting, pottery, bamboo, jewelry, books and accessories. Designers exhibiting include Wanju Kim, Max Lamb, Antoli, Lars Frideen, and VAAS.

MOUKI

29 Chiltern St, City of Westminster, London, +44 20 7224 4010
https://moukimou.com/
NEIGHBORHOOD: Marylebone
This concept boutique offers unique and exclusive treasures from around the world. Here you'll find a selection of ready-to-wear, jewelry and beauty and lifestyle products.

NELLY DUFF

156 Columbia Rd, London, +44 20 7033 9683
www.nellyduff.com
NEIGHBORHOOD: Shoreditch
Located in the heart of London's East End, this gallery offers exhibitions of editions and original works from emerging artists of the Street, Tattoo and Graphic art world. This gallery was one

of the first to exhibit Street Art internationally. Here you'll find exhibitions and available prints by artists like Eine and Pure Evil.

PAXTON & WHITFIELD

93 Jermyn St, London, +44 20 7930 0259
www.paxtonandwhitfield.co.uk/
NEIGHBORHOOD: Piccadilly
Known for serving as cheesemonger to Queen Victoria, this 200-year-old shop boasts an impressive selection of the world's greatest artisanal cheeses, especially British and French labels. Here you'll also find ham, pâté, condiments, accessories, sauces, preserves, wine, and fresh sandwiches.

ROCOCO CHOCOLATES

3 Moxton St, London, +44 20 7935 7780
www.rococochocolates.com
NEIGHBORHOOD: Marylebone
Chocolate lovers come to Rococo chocolates for its impressive supply of chocolate flavors, truffles, unusual chocolate items and gifts. The master chocolatiers also offer workshops and tastings at their chocolate school.

SUNSPEL
7 Redchurch St, London, +44 20 7739 9729
www.sunspel.com
NEIGHBORHOOD: Soho
Menswear shop founded by Thomas A. Hill who had the idea to
make clothing from beautiful fabrics. This beautiful classic
brand specializes in quality underwear, T-shirts and polo shirts.
Also available are trousers, shorts, outerwear and swimwear.
Ladies fashions are

TRUNK CLOTHIERS
8 Chiltern St, London, +44 20 3030 5100
www.trunkclothiers.com
NEIGHBORHOOD: Marylebone
This cozy neighborhood shop features an impressive collection
of menswear and accessories from Japan, Italy, Sweden, the UK
and US. Here you'll find classic quality fashions and impeccable
service.

TRUNK LABS
8 Chiltern St, London, +44 20 3030 5100
www.trunkclothiers.com
NEIGHBORHOOD: Marylebone
Trunk LABS is a men's accessories shop featuring an
impressive selection of luggage, bags and shoes. Here you'll
find ties, belts, grooming products, stationary, eyewear, home
wares, furniture, and leather goods.

VINTAGE/SECONDHAND SHOPS

SHELTER/LITTLE VENICE BOUTIQUE
31 Clifton Rd, London, +44 20 7286 4671
https://england.shelter.org.uk/support_us/shops/little_venice
Little Venice boutique charity shop sells designer, high-end
street fashions as well as vintage one-of-a-kind pieces at greatly
discounted prices. Great place to donate your designer duds.

TRIAD
70-72 Kilburn High Rd, North Maida Vale, London, +44 20
7328 3912
www.traid.org.uk/
Charity selling secondhand clothes, aiming to improve workers'
lives in the global textile industry.

VINTAGE THREADS
69 Neal St, London, +44 7795 389292
https://vintage-threads.com/
Great shopping. Here you'll find a selection of vintage fashions,
accessories, jewelry, and designer bags. Check out their sales.

INDEX

M

N

O

P

Z